The Nonstop Garden

The Nonstop Garden

A Step-by-Step Guide to Smart Plant Choices and Four-Season Designs

Stephanie Cohen & Jennifer Benner

TIMBER PRESS
Portland • London

Frontispiece: *Alchemilla mollis* (left of center), *Nepeta* 'Six Hills Giant' (left of center), *Allium* 'Globemaster' (bottom right, top center, top left), *Picea pungens* 'Montgomery' (bottom right, top center, top left), and *Salvia ×sylvestris* 'Mainacht' (syn. *S. ×sylvestris* 'May Night', bottom right, right of center, top left). Taken at the Ginsburg Garden.

Photographs, including those reprinted with permission of *Fine Gardening* magazine and the Taunton Press, Inc., are by Jennifer Benner unless otherwise indicated.

Watercolor illustrations © Karla Beatty.

Garden plans created by the authors and drawn by Marjorie Leggitt.

Published in 2010 by Timber Press, Inc.

The Haseltine Building
133 S.W. Second Avenue, Suite 450
Portland, Oregon 97204-3527
www.timberpress.com

2 The Quadrant
135 Salusbury Road
London NW6 6RJ
www.timberpress.co.uk

ISBN-13: 978-0-88192-951-5

Printed in China

Library of Congress Cataloging-in-Publication Data
Cohen, Stephanie, 1937-
  The nonstop garden : a step-by-step guide to smart plant choices and four-season designs / Stephanie Cohen and Jennifer Benner.
      p. cm.
  Includes bibliographical references and index.
  ISBN 978-0-88192-951-5
  1. Gardens—Design. 2. Plants, Ornamental—Seasonal variations. I. Benner, Jennifer. II. Title.
  SB472.45.C63 2010
  712'.6—dc22   2009046596

A catalog record for this book is also available from the British Library.

To my family—my husband, who has tolerated my fixation with plants for more than fifty years; my children, Abby, Doug, and Rachel, who as children were dragged to gardens and arboretums, and didn't run away from home; and my daughter-in-law, Suzanne, who has presented me with two favorite flowers, my grandchildren, Chelsea and Devyn, whom I hope to convert to gardening as their hobby and passion.

—*Stephanie Cohen*

To my husband, Brent. I could not have worked on this project without you, all the pots of coffee you made, and all the help you provided in keeping "things" going. In between all of life's weeds, walking around the garden with you to discover what is new is the best part of my day.

—*Jennifer Benner*

Contents

Garden Designs

Acknowledgments

I would like to thank all the staff at Timber Press. It is important to have an editor who believes in you and gives his all to help you succeed. Tom Fischer is a paragon among editors. He gave me the confidence to keep writing, and for that I am truly grateful. I would also like to thank Nancy Ondra, who encouraged me to start writing and coauthored my other two books. Thank you to one of my best buddies, Sharee Solow, a horticulturist and great designer, for all her help and technical assistance. Thanks, too, to Rob Cardillo, my favorite photographer, for answering all of our photography queries.

I would like to thank all those in the horticulture field that have been so supportive all these years, especially the Perennial Plant Association. I am also grateful to all the gardeners who have listened, written, and communicated to me how much they appreciate my work and how it has helped them become better gardeners. Last but not least, thank you to Jennifer Benner, my former editor at *Fine Gardening*, who was willing to collaborate with me to bring you this exciting new book. She is beginning her writing career, and I look forward to her future accomplishments. It takes a lot of people and help to get a book to press—if I have forgotten anyone, my excuse is that I'm an official senior!

—STEPHANIE COHEN

Thank you to Timber Press and all the talented people who worked so hard on this project, including Tom Fischer, Eve Goodman, Mindy Fitch, Michael Dempsey, and my amazing coauthor, Stephanie Cohen. Thank you to all the garden owners, designers, and public gardens who allowed me to photograph their spaces and generously provided details about their plantings. Thank you to all the horticulturists who shared their knowledge and provided assistance, especially Debby Bennett, Russ Buhrow, Janet Egger, Michelle Gervais, Dan Heims, Jon Peter, Andrew Schulman, Steve Silk, Ilene Sternberg, and Bill Thomas. Thank you also to John Elsley, Bailey Nurseries, Brent and Becky's Bulbs, *Fine Gardening*, J. Frank Schmidt and Son, Monrovia, North Creek Nurseries, Spring Meadow Nursery, Sunny Border Nurseries, Terra Nova Nurseries, and White Flower Farm for offering help with additional photos and plant information.

I am grateful to all the wonderful gardening teachers I have had over the years, from my former colleagues and oodles of authors at *Fine Gardening* to the Nantucket crew (particularly Mike Glowacki and Mike Misurelli) to my mentors from Ohio State (especially Denise Adams). You have all played a role in making me the gardener I am today.

Thank you to my incredibly supportive family and friends; sorry I went missing for so long. I am especially appreciative of my cheering section—my father, Dave, and sister, Beth; Beth and Steve Agren; Steve Aitken; Wendy Bowes; the Clancys; Andy Engel and Pat Steed; Leslie Lewis and the CFPA crew; Missy and Brian Lucas; Rita Randolph; Lee Schneller Sligh; and Virginia Small. Last but certainly not least, thank you to my mother, Judy, and grandmothers, Essie, Betty, and Alice—the gardeners who got me started. I am honored to have inherited a green thumb and cherish the fond memories I have of spending time in your gardens. I wish you were all still here to cultivate new memories with me in mine.

—JENNIFER BENNER

Introduction

The purpose of this book is to show you how to build an integrated garden (including trees, shrubs, perennials, bulbs, annuals, tropicals, edibles, and vines) with year-round interest—what we call a "nonstop garden." Nonstop gardens are better gardens because they require less maintenance, provide continual beauty, allow more creativity, and encourage diversity.

We begin with the nuts and bolts, including easy design strategies, but quickly move on to plants, which when it comes down to it are what ultimately make or break the nonstop garden. After all, although elements such as ornaments, paths, and arbors play a big role, these little slices of heaven are mostly made up of plants. The great thing about plants being key players is that they can easily be changed. If a plant is not working, get rid of it. If a plant dies, no big deal—get a new one. If a plant flourishes, get another one. Part of the garden journey is trial and error. Of course, it always feels better if you win more than you lose. With that in mind, we offer chapters filled with plant recommendations based on our forty years of collective gardening experience. The plants we recommend are those we consider top-notch; all offer stunning beauty and require minimal maintenance.

The plant entries provided throughout the book are headed by the plant's common name followed by the scientific name, starting with maple (*Acer* species and cultivars) in chapter 3, "Trees and Shrubs." Each plant entry begins with information about hardiness zones, peak seasons, and the conditions required for the plant to grow well.

The zones indicate the range in which you can expect plants in that particular genus or species to be cold hardy. For more information, see "Hardiness Zones" at the end of the book.

The peak seasons refer to the timing of the plant's star performance. In the case of maples, these are listed as "Fall (foliage), winter (bark, stems)." This information is essential when choosing plants that you want to provide year-round interest. For your convenience we have also included a seasonal peak plant performance table at the end of the book.

Finally, in addition to describing recommended species and cultivars, each plant entry gives you a heads-up on any particulars you may want to know about cultivation as well as pests, diseases, or other problems the plant is likely (or unlikely) to face.

When choosing plants, we highly recommend exploring native options—after all, these plants have been happily growing in our environment for thousands of years without any help from humans. As plantaholic gardeners, we also enjoy exotic plants, but only if they behave themselves. Always be mindful of invasive species, and know that not all plants play nicely in all parts of the world. Check your state listings before introducing a

new plant to your garden. See "Invasive Plants" at the end of the book for a list of species to keep on your radar.

To show you some choice plants in action, we have also included ten easy-to-follow garden designs: a winter garden, a wildlife garden, a native garden, a woodland garden, a cool-colored garden, a garden for wet sites, a gold-colored garden, a vibrant-colored garden, a scented garden, and a parking strip (or "inferno strip") garden. And we discuss the finishing touches, from ornamentation and containers to structures such as walkways, fences, trellises, and furniture, all of which create additional interest in the nonstop garden.

Nonstop gardening is an approach that can be enjoyed by everyone. Whether you are new to gardening or have a seasoned green thumb, these practical pointers and plants will help heighten interest in any outdoor surrounding, big or small.

PART ONE

THE NUTS AND BOLTS

Reliable plant choices with interesting flowers, foliage, and textures provide the best show for the least amount of effort. Clockwise from top: *Amsonia hubrichtii*, *Picea pungens* 'Montgomery', *Iris laevigata* 'Variegata', and *Gomphrena* 'Strawberry Fields'. Taken at The New York Botanical Garden.

1

The Benefits of the Nonstop Garden

Gardening books do not usually mince words; they get right to the point. This seems kind of odd since gardens have such interesting stories to tell. They are constantly changing and evolving, on their own and by a gardener's hand. They have a lot to say and a lot to teach.

Diversity is a key component of the nonstop garden. The greater the mix of seasonal plants, the more you will enjoy your garden throughout the year. Taken at the Leva Garden.

For this book, let us start out like this: Once upon a time, more then twenty-five years ago, there was a gardener named Stephanie. She was a new gardener. She was a perennial gardener—a purist through and through. No plants with woody stems or less-than-hardy dispositions made it past her gate. And like her perennial friends, she displayed her "Friends Don't Let Friends Buy Annuals" bumper sticker with pride and disdain. As time went on, Stephanie continuously wrestled with and rearranged her perennial plantings, wondering why they had

no oomph and just did not jive.

So she visited other gardens and began taking notes. Much to her dismay, she realized that perennials play more nicely with others. Stephanie had a change of heart and has been mixing perennials, woody plants, herbs, annuals, and tropicals in her garden ever since.

It is no wonder that we often start our gardening journey as plant segregationists. We are hardwired that way. We began cultivating the earth out of necessity, for food. Plots of this and plots of that were the most efficient way to go.

Choosing from a larger plant palette allows you to be more creative and fill seasonal gaps. Taken at Linden Hill Gardens.

Unfortunately, this approach trickled into our ornamental gardening, relegating annuals to the annual garden, herbs to the herb bed, tropicals to containers, and trees and shrubs to foundation plantings. Thankfully, in the last half century we have seen the errors of our ways. Mixed beds and borders are popping up almost as quickly as McMansions, which is not a bad thing. This planting style offers more creative opportunities, encourages diversity, and requires less maintenance. Best of all, mixed beds and borders open the door to the nonstop garden, giving us year-round interest.

While broad ornamental plant groups like perennials and annuals do offer a wide selection of choices on their own, the options are just a drop in the bucket compared to what is possible when all the groups are pulled together. Tall, short, wide, thin, flowers, fruit, yellow, blue—the list of notable characteristics is endless. Embracing a diverse mix of plants really is the best way to create dynamic plantings. Plus, when it comes to creativity, choosing to grow only one group of plants is like shooting yourself in the foot. An expanded plant palette gives you more options to play with as you work to create interesting combinations. Bringing broad plant groups together allows you to build well-rounded mixed beds and borders, brimming with plants that provide engaging color, form, texture, and structure.

Annuals, perennials, woody plants, and tropicals—every plant group brings different strengths to the table. Perennials such as geraniums are great for seasonal blooms that return year after year. Annuals may only be around for one gardening season, but plants like mini petunia (*Calibrachoa* cultivars) earn their keep with loads of flowers from start to finish. Tropicals add va-va-voom to plantings with their bold features. Even though they are tender in many parts of the United States, showstoppers like cannas (*Canna* species and cultivars) offer a summer's worth of fantastically large leaves and vivid blooms. It is hard to beat trees and shrubs when it comes to structure. These plants are the bones of the garden. Without them, plantings would fall flat— just like us without our bones (yuck, not a pretty sight). In the end, each group is indispensable in the mixed border.

Probably the greatest thing about an expanded plant palette is that it provides an opportunity to have something going on in the garden during all four seasons. Several times each year the garden just seems down and out, such as early spring when the ground is stark and winter's chill still lingers in the air, or the dog days of summer when the heat and humidity are too intense for man, plant, or beast. Each season has its unique conditions and challenges, some worse than others. Thank goodness for those plants that do their thing at times of the year when many others are taking a snooze. Early spring is not so gloomy thanks to bright and cheery bulbs. The roasting days of July are so much more bearable with lush tropicals, annuals, grasses, and summer-flowering shrubs that can take the heat. Where would we be in autumn without the rich fall colors and vibrant fruits of trees and shrubs, or the last of the late-flowering perennials? Winter would indeed be quite dreary if it were not for the subtle, artful beauty of the bones of the garden—evergreen foliage, tree bark, persistent berries and seed-heads, and oddly shaped trees and shrubs accented by a blanket of snow. Put these plants together, and you have yourself a nonstop garden.

RUBBING ELBOWS WITH NATURE

People are not the only ones who appreciate good mixed borders, which are a hit with wildlife, too. We sometimes take critters for granted, but when they are absent, we sure take notice. Take our former perennial-only gardener, Stephanie, for example. When she first moved to her current home twelve years ago, the property was dotted with mostly builders'-grade evergreens. It was about as exciting as watching paint dry, and she quickly noticed that few birds, butterflies, or toads were to be found. It was a stagnant landscape and certainly provided very little wildlife habitat. "If you build it, they will come" became her motto, and she went to work building a diversified garden. Within the first year, twelve different butterfly species became regular visitors. Today, everything from dragonflies to frogs, turkeys, and foxes can be found taking respite in Stephanie's garden.

Without wildlife and all living creatures, we would be in big trouble. Everybody, even the tiniest soil microbe, has a role in the earth's ecological system and ultimately impacts the health of our air and water. Everyone is dependent on one another for sustenance and to keep the ecological engine moving. If a few members of the team are taken out of the game, it can have a negative impact on the entire team. With natural habitat disappearing at an alarming rate, wildlife

is running out of places to go. It is more important than ever for us to do what we can to provide wildlife with alternate places to live, such as mixed borders and landscapes. This enriches not only our environmental and physical health but also our minds and wellbeing, allowing people, young and old, to learn about and connect with nature's wonders. The live show is still far more meaningful than the shows found on television or computers.

Diverse plantings offer habitat for wildlife neighbors.

LESS WORK, MORE PLAY

Who does not love a good shortcut? If you were given the option to get from A to B faster, with less effort and better results, would you not take it? Skeptics might say

Devoting more space to mixed plantings and less space to lawns helps to minimize maintenance and conserve resources. Taken at the Cohen Garden.

no, thinking it too good to be true. When it comes to low-maintenance mixed beds, nothing could be further from the truth—especially when compared to lawns. Turf does offer a place for pets and children to scamper about, but perhaps we do not need so much of it. Mixed plantings are engaging to people and wildlife. They also require less water, fertilizer, and maintenance than a flat, boring expanse of green, which allows you to devote more time and resources to stopping and smelling the roses.

Typical lawns require at least an inch of water per week during the growing season, while carefully selected low-maintenance trees, shrubs, and herbaceous plants can live on the water Mother Nature gives them once they are established. It is widely recommended that lawns receive at least four fertilizer applications a year, whereas most low-maintenance ornamentals are happy with one feeding of compost or a naturally derived fertilizer each year.

Depending on the climate, a lawn must be mowed at least every two weeks. The frequency can shoot up to every three to four days in the rainy season or for regularly irrigated lawns. In addition, depending on the size of the lawn and type of lawn mower, each mowing can take a few hours—not to mention the gas needed to fuel the machine. This may sound fine to people who love to mow, but many others would rather be doing something else with their time and resources.

Perennial borders can sometimes be just as labor intensive, requiring a fair amount of deadheading, weeding, and dividing. An established low-maintenance mixed border, on the other hand, only needs attention maybe every two weeks for some light weeding and minor pruning. This could take several hours, too, depending on the size of the border, but it does not have to be done all at once like the lawn. Spreading out a few hours of work over a couple of weeks definitely sounds more appealing than having to put your nose to the grindstone for a few hours every three to four days. Makes ornamental grasses look far more appealing than turf, that is for sure.

MINIMIZING HEADACHES

Another nice thing about diversified plantings is that they help to minimize insects and diseases. Some troublemakers, like aphids, are not gourmets but gourmands, snacking on anything and everything. They can be a problem whether you have a mixed border or not. Many insects, however, will only feed on certain plants. The small orange aphid just eats plants in the milkweed family (Asclepiadaceae). Unless you have an entire garden of milkweed (*Asclepias* species and cultivars), having an infestation of this or a similarly selective insect will not keep you up at night wondering whether your garden will be there in the morning.

Plant diseases work in a similar way. Some plants are more susceptible than others to certain diseases, such as the common fungal disease powdery mildew. *Phlox* (*Phlox paniculata* and cultivars), lungwort (*Pulmonaria* species and cultivars), bee balm (*Monarda* species and cultivars), and a few other perennials are particularly prone to this malady. So unless you are planning a mildew version of the renowned Sissinghurst Castle Garden in England, avoid planting a

garden of just highly susceptible plants. The more you diversify, the happier and healthier your garden will be. Monocultures are just asking for trouble. If you are ever tempted to plant just one kind, think back to the elms (*Ulmus americana*) and chestnuts (*Castanea dentata*) that used to line small-town streets in the United States. When Dutch elm disease and chestnut blight hit, our beautiful street trees were wiped out.

The benefits of mixed beds and borders are astounding. Whether you are new to gardening or a seasoned veteran, this is the perfect way to dig in with less effort. Gardening should be fun. The key is to garden smarter, not harder.

Using a mix of plants will prevent your entire garden from being annihilated when a problem arises.

2 Easy Design Strategies That Work

Even the most experienced gardeners will admit that putting a garden together is not a piece of cake. You not only have to contend with site conditions and climatic challenges but also must assemble and arrange a group of plants that perform well and look good together.

Select a mix of plants that add depth and structure to provide heightened interest throughout the year. Taken at the Diemer Garden.

This process has left gardeners scratching their heads for eons. With a few key design principles in your back pocket, however, you can be well on your way to creating pleasing plantings. As with fashion and interior décor trends, garden styles have come, gone, and returned over the last couple of centuries, but fundamental design strategies have stood the test of time. The reason? That is easy: because they work.

For some, just the words "principles" and "strategies" are a turnoff. We creative types do not want boring, stuffy rules interfering with our artfulness. Once we warm up to the idea, however, we usually see that they are more of an aid than a hindrance. Garden design strategies are tools to success. Putting them to good use is hardly selling out. We can still march to the beat of our own drums and explore our creativity with the choices we make. The plants, colors, forms, and accessories that we select allow us to express ourselves and convey desired themes. Strategies just help us to put these elements into an attractive arrangement instead of a jumbled mess.

BUILD YOUR GARDEN ROOM BY ROOM

The easiest way to begin building mixed borders is by dividing your landscape into bite-sized spaces. Gardens always seem less daunting when you break them down into manageable areas. They also seem more welcoming, engaging, and intimate for those who visit. The simplest way to divide a garden is to look at each area like a room in a house. Garden rooms are by no means a revolutionary idea—pretty much every gardening book talks about

them—but they are very effective design elements.

Start by pinpointing the function of each area. Decide whether you want a place to entertain, work, relax, bathe, and so forth. Do you have a yen for an outdoor kitchen equipped with a fresh supply of herbs and veggies? Do you have the perfect shady nook to hide in or a sunny place to grow, cut, and arrange flowers? Just as interior kitchens, living rooms, dining rooms, studies, and mudrooms serve a purpose, so do garden rooms. A back patio or deck is a great central location for an entertainment area, while a spa or water feature can be the heart of a relaxation room. Garden rooms may not always be as clear-cut as the rooms in a home, but as you get deeper into developing the concept, they do become more obvious.

If your landscape already has established garden rooms, consider whether they need some remodeling. Garden rooms are more comfortable when they

Tackling a garden room by room and focusing on each room's function helps to make the design process less daunting. Taken at the Silk Garden.

To match the right plants to your site, take note of where the light hits in your garden throughout the day and choose plants accordingly. Taken at Linden Hill Gardens.

have distinct or implied perimeters and thresholds. These elements help to define the space for visitors, giving them the lay of the land and indicating where to enter and exit. Perimeters can be as apparent as a hedge or as subtle as a change in materials, such as the point where a patio butts up to a lawn. Likewise, thresholds can take many forms, from an ornate gate to a simple stepping-stone. Whether you are starting with a blank slate or an established landscape, consider putting garden rooms into play. Once you have them mapped out, it will be easier to begin selecting plants for the mixed plantings in your nonstop garden.

GET TO KNOW YOUR SITE

Even though we learned at an early age that a square peg will not fit into a round hole, this basic lesson is worth revisiting, especially when it comes to gardening. You will have the best outcome by working with your site, not against it. You may despise your dry, hot, sunny plot or damp, shady nook, but it is what it is. Unless you are Donald Trump and can afford to crane in a mature shade tree or move a house, there is usually very little you can do about the site you are dealt. The best thing to do is capitalize on your site's strengths and realize its limitations.

Choosing plants that do not grow well in your site's conditions, whether it is because you are in denial or just do not know any better, will send you down the road to heartache and failure. Always follow the cardinal rule: put the right plant in the right place. Get to know your site, do your homework, and choose plants that will thrive in the light and soil that you have to offer. Of course, also allow

room for a little experimentation. Sometimes plants let us get away with bending the rules slightly. When they do not, their unfortunate demise provides a great excuse to go shopping for more plants.

START WITH A PLAN

Before a shovel even touches the ground, make sure you sketch a plan. It may be a dreaded four-letter word, but a plan will keep you from getting distracted, overwhelmed, and veering off track. Having a plan does not mean you cannot change your mind midstream; it just provides a good road map to get you headed in the

right direction. Consider it like making dinner. You have a recipe to follow, but once you begin you may find you need to make ingredient or pan substitutions, depending on your mood and what you have in the cupboard.

There is also no rule that says a plan has to be a major work of art. How many of us can really draw? Plans can be simple sketches of labeled lines, squares, circles, and X's, used to lay out our plantings and their location. You can create a plan for your entire property, each garden room, specific beds, or all three. The more specific you get, the simpler the execution

A common theme, such as ornamental grasses, can be threaded throughout beds and garden rooms to create a cohesive whole. Taken at Chanticleer Garden.

For greatest impact, arrange plants in groupings and in random, more natural-looking configurations. Taken at the Hall-Behrens Garden.

will be. It is up to you—just grab a pencil and some paper and get something down. If you still feel intimidated by drawing, make the process super easy (and fun) by drawing an outline of your planting beds, grabbing some old plant catalogs, cutting out the pictures, and arranging and sticking them on the page.

Even though it is easier to design a garden by breaking it up into sections or rooms, you still want the entire garden to feel like a collective whole. You can do this by threading similar elements throughout each room. Repetition is a strong yet subtle visual tool that helps disjointed areas feel united. It can take many forms, as many as your imagination will allow. For example, it can be present in the structural materials you use. If you have a wooden deck, perhaps you choose to build a wooden arbor in one room and include a wooden bench in another. Likewise, the same bluestone could be used to create your patio and all the paths that wind through every room in the garden. Or perhaps you would like your common denominator to be flower spikes or the color burgundy. Choosing your favorite flower form, color, or plant and weaving it through each room in your garden is an excellent way to bring it all together.

CHOOSE THE RIGHT PLANTS

First, avoid impulsive plant purchases. For many gardeners, buying plants is an addiction like a sweet tooth. We cannot stop at just one, and we are always on the lookout for our next tasty treat. In the heat of the moment, we often end up throwing all rationale out the window and purchasing jaw-dropping plants that are inappropriate for our garden conditions or that do not work in our design schemes. This leads to overcrowded, sickly plantings or a stockpile of homeless plants. Although it may be difficult, it is best to try to curb that appetite and only hit the garden center or catalogs with a plan in mind and a need for specific plants. You can allow yourself to indulge a little. Leave some space for the "If I can't have it, I'm going to die" plants you may come across throughout the season. Also, do not fully commit to hardy plants that return year after year. By designating space for annuals, biennials, and tropicals, you give yourself some shopping trips to look forward to each gardening season.

Impulsive plant purchases can also lead to a garden that looks like it was designed with a blender. It has no rhyme or reason, just a whole lot of one of this and one of that. To create the greatest impact, display varieties in larger drifts and take direction from nature. Place your groups in random configurations, not straight rows, and plant them in odd numbers (groups of three, five, seven) to give them a more natural appearance. The exception to the rule is specimen or focal point plants. Every planting deserves a show-off, and in this case one is not a lowly number. When it comes to extremely large or bold plants, one is often all you need. Just be sure to feature these plants in moderation to achieve the biggest wow factor. Remember that less is more. Try to limit the total number of different species or selections per planting. Planning a minimum of 4 to 6 square feet per plant variety is a good place to start.

Pay attention to size. Trends may come and go, but when you are talking gardens, the layered look is always in.

Mother Nature has been strutting this classic style since time began. Just take a look at a naturalized woodland made up of tall skyscraper trees that are underscored by understory trees and shrubs and a lush carpet of herbaceous plants. Whether your bed is big or small, take cues from nature and create dynamic layers of plants to establish structure and depth. Structure keeps a garden from looking one-dimensional. It also keeps the garden in scale with its surroundings. A mixed border made up of 3-foot-tall plants would look wimpy and out of place running along the base of a two-story house or barn. Include a small, 15-foot-tall tree and a mix of 4- to 10-foot-tall shrubs and perennials, and that border will look right at home.

When selecting plants, focus on foliage. Although foliage may seem like a plain Jane when compared to flowers, it is one of the most important features on a plant. Flowers are transient, while leaves can last up to two, three, or four seasons. If a plant has "yuck" foliage right after flowering, as many spring perennials do, it might be best to plant it in your compost pile. Choose plants with leaves that dazzle for at least a good portion of the year. There are many options out there. Foliage comes in all shapes and sizes, from long, 1-inch-wide grass blades to huge 3-foot-round pads. Leaf colors seem endless, coming in shades of green, yellow, silver, blue, red, and everything in between. Variegated leaves like those found on many hostas (*Hosta* species and cultivars) can be real showstoppers. When used in moderation, they punctuate the mixed border with their unique charm. Plants with foliage that changes seasonally really take the cake. The glossy green foliage of large

Size does matter. Large-scale, upright plants help to add needed structure without overwhelming an adjacent patio. Taken at the Leva Garden.

fothergilla (*Fothergilla major*) makes a beautiful foil throughout the gardening season. Come autumn, however, the leaves shed their reticence and take center stage with a spectacular display of orange, red, and yellow. Evergreen plants like hollies (*Ilex* species and cultivars) and hellebores (*Helleborus* species and cultivars) are nothing to shake a stick at either, typically offering handsome foliage 365 days a year.

Foliage also plays a big role in a garden's visual palette of texture. Each plant has two basic levels of texture: the tactile nature of its flowers, stems, and leaves, and the visual presence of its overall appearance. While tactical texture is often experienced in the garden, visual texture is the primary textural concern when it comes to design. Visual texture is categorized as either coarse, medium, or fine. Think of coarse texture as a walnut that has been broken in half, medium texture as those pieces chopped into quarters, and fine texture as those portions minced into small slivers. From a gardening perspective, plants like bold-leaved bananas (*Musa* species and cultivars), lush viburnums (*Viburnum* species and cultivars), and slender fountain grasses (*Pennisetum* species and cultivars) are coarse, medium, and fine, respectively. How plants interact texturally is just as important as how they relate chromatically. In a mixed border, an assortment of coarse, medium, and fine textures is the key to creating dynamic visual depth. Placing contrasting textures next to each other helps plants to "pop" instead of getting lost in the crowd.

Even though there is something interesting and beautiful about every plant, it does not follow that every plant is garden-worthy. To create a low-maintenance nonstop garden with extended interest, you must be discriminating with your plant choices. Grabbing plants willy-nilly is not the way to go. Obviously the plants you choose should match your conditions and be largely trouble free. They should also have robust dispositions and hold their own once established. Do not enlist a lot of prima donnas like hybrid tea roses (*Rosa* cultivars) that demand coddling and frequent pest and disease treatments. A better choice would be a plant like catmint (*Nepeta* species and cultivars), which needs maybe an annual feeding and pruning, occasional deadheading or dividing, and perhaps a drink during dry spells.

When making your selections, check out native plants, too. These vigorous gems already like your conditions and are the cornerstones of any sustainable landscape. Exotic workhorses are a-okay, but be sure they are not invasive and do not have the potential to negatively impact the environment. And by all means do not turn your nose up at the average Joes. The local garden society might find plants like impatiens (*Impatiens* species and cultivars) to be a little too pedestrian, but if they work, who cares?

Finally, get the most bang for your buck. Regardless of their origins, the best nonstop garden plants are tough and have a lot of character. Do not fill your roster with a lot of one-hit wonders, such as columbine (*Aquilegia* species and cultivars), that seduce you with their blooms at the nursery and then disappear after the flowers fizzle out. Likewise, do not get carried away and load up on plants that

Plants with intriguing foliage provide lots of interest after flowers are long gone. Taken at Terra Nova Nurseries.

are only in bloom during a trip to the garden center—a good marketing and sales tactic that will lead to a garden that only shines at certain times of the year. Instead, pick plants that will look good for long periods and feature several different attributes at various times of the year. Perennials and tropicals with attractive foliage and blooms, like coral bells (*Heuchera* species and cultivars) and cannas (*Canna* species and cultivars), are at the top of the list, as are trees and shrubs with handsome flowers, leaves, fruit, and stems, like dogwoods (*Cornus* species and cultivars).

That is not to say you should avoid ephemeral plants altogether. While they may be fleeting, they do help to round out the mixed border, offering seasonal color when the main attractions are off duty. Seasonal workhorse bulbs like daffodils (*Narcissus* species and cultivars), ornamental onions (*Allium* species and cultivars), and camas (*Camassia* species and cultivars) are great because they offer colorful blooms, multiply rapidly, and grow whether you help them or not. Choosing a mix of all-star plants with substance will provide optimum plant diversity, maximizing one of the basic tenets of nonstop gardening.

Give plants with long-lasting or multiple seasonal attributes, such as blooms, berries, and variegated foliage, a prominent position. Taken at The New York Botanical Garden.

Recipe for Success

Building a mixed border is a lot like preparing your favorite soup. You start with a foundation of broth and then add ample proportions of ingredients like vegetables, noodles, and herbs. Everyone has his or her own variation on the recipe, which gives the end result a flavor that suits individual tastes. In the mixed border, start with trees and shrubs as your foundation, or broth. Then begin adding your flavorful ingredients—perennials, bulbs, annuals, tropicals, vines, and maybe a few edibles. This chart represents a good basic proportional plant recipe, which can be easily be tweaked for taste.

30% trees and shrubs

30% perennials

20% annuals and tropicals

10% bulbs

5% vines

5% veggies and herbs

PART TWO

THE MAIN ATTRACTIONS

Woody plants and hardy perennials like *Hydrangea* 'Preziosa' and *Polygonatum odoratum* 'Variegatum' serve as building blocks for the nonstop garden. Taken at Chanticleer Garden.

3 Trees and Shrubs

The majestic trees found in our native landscapes have made more than a few jaws drop in their day. It is hard not to be impressed by towering canopies several stories high and enormous trunks that you cannot even wrap your arms around.

Cercis canadensis adds remarkable form and seasonal attributes to mixed plantings. Taken at The New York Botanical Garden.

While most of us do not have the space (or time) to enjoy cultivating these huge botanical wonders, we can grow some of the more appropriately sized trees and shrubs, which provide significant impact in the nonstop garden. Trees and shrubs are the ultimate structural plants. They create the framework of the garden, offering architectural stems, branches, and forms that are present in spring, summer, autumn, and winter. They can even wow us with beautiful blooms, attractive leaves, interesting fruit, and handsome bark.

Because woody plants require more space and can take longer to mature than herbaceous plants, it is a good idea to pick and plant your trees and shrubs before planting anything else. It is much easier to place them in beds and borders when you do not have to worry about stepping on or disturbing existing annuals, perennials, bulbs, or tropicals.

There is no shortage of trees and shrubs out there. Look for options that offer long-lasting or multiple seasonal attributes. When it comes to woody plants, deciduous selections provide the most bling. Do not forget to throw a few evergreens in the mix, however, which will settle in as reliable, year-round backbones in the garden.

TOP-NOTCH TREES

Trees add dimension to a scene with their strong vertical forms and provide ornamental character with their seasonal details. They are a useful design tool, anchoring a planting scheme. More importantly, they serve as liaisons or connector points between more large-scale items like buildings or bigger, more mature trees and shrubs or lower-growing perennials.

Because trees are not all that easy to move once established, and because they come with a moderately expensive price tag, placing them in the landscape should not be taken lightly. Do your homework and find a specimen that is suited to your conditions and exhibits characteristics that will enhance your garden. The following tried-and-true options are small in stature as far as trees go, but big on impact, making them great choices for restricted spaces.

Maple

Acer species and cultivars, zones 3 to 9
Spring to fall (foliage), winter (bark, stems)

Full sun to partial shade; moist, well-drained, average soil

No doubt, *Acer* is one of the most recognized tree genera in the northern hemisphere. It is often the first tree leaf we learn and collect in grade school. Revered for their magnificent foliage, especially in fall, maples are a fairly diverse group, ranging in size, form, and leaf characteristics. While the large shade-tree varieties like red maple (*A. rubrum* and cultivars, zones 3 to 9) provide impact in expansive landscape settings, they are a little too big for mixed beds and foundation plantings. Luckily, lots of smaller options offer extended seasonal interest.

Paperbark maple (*Acer griseum* and cultivars, zones 4 to 8) and three-flower maple (*A. triflorum*, zones 4 to 7) lead the charge for smaller plants with attractive exfoliating bark and striking red fall color. Both grow 20 to 30 feet tall and

Acer palmatum 'Bloodgood'. Taken at Hollister House Garden.

usually about half as wide with an upright, roundish habit, sporting the typical trifoliate maple leaves. They make excellent specimen trees in mixed plantings, as does trident maple (*A. buergerianum* and cultivars, zones 5 to 9), which reaches about the same size with multiple stems and features gold to red fall color. Amur maple (*A. tataricum* subsp. *ginnala* and cultivars, syn. *A. ginnala*, zones 3 to 7) is another lovely multistemmed option that rarely exceeds 20 feet tall.

Alternatively, Japanese maples (*Acer palmatum* cultivars, zones 5 to 8) are wildly popular due to their colorful leaves. The dissected, sometimes lacy foliage comes in shades of green, yellow, and red in summer, usually turning an intense yellow, orange, or red in autumn. Japanese maples can grow anywhere from 6 to 25 feet tall with various upright to mounding structural forms, depending on the variety. There are also variegated selections. Like most maples, their tiny, late-spring flowers are interesting if you look closely, but go relatively unnoticed.

Maples are mostly trouble free. Any insect or disease problems are largely species-dependent and are more common with the big, big trees. The best time to prune maples is either when they are dormant in winter or after they have started actively growing in late spring. Avoid cutting them in early spring when their buds are plump and the sap is flowing.

Serviceberry

Amelanchier species and cultivars, zones 2 to 9
Spring (flowers), fall (foliage, fruit)

Full sun to partial shade; moist to moderately dry, well-drained, fertile, acidic soil

This genus, largely native to North America, offers up a hardy mix of small trees or large shrubs, depending on your perspective, with lots of seasonal interest. In spring serviceberries hit the ground running with abundant, star-shaped, white flowers that can open to nearly an inch across. Around the same time, the leaves often start out with a bronze or silver cast, sprouting from each plant's multiple stems. The leaves age to medium green as they soak up the summer sun. The flowers are shortly followed by juicy, red cranberry-sized fruit that ripens to dark purple. The fruit usually does not last long since it is quickly gobbled up by birds and mammals, including humans. In autumn the foliage steals the show as it turns brilliant shades of yellow, orange, and red.

Allegheny serviceberry (*Amelanchier laevis* and cultivars, zones 4 to 8) can reach 15 to 30 feet tall and about half as wide in cultivation and produces reddish new leaves. Downy serviceberry (*A. arborea* and cultivars, zones 4 to 9) is a very similar species that will grow farther south and to about the same size. Its new leaves unfurl with a silver pubescence, and the fruit is said to be not so tasty. Apple serviceberry (*A.* ×*grandiflora* cultivars, zones 4 to 9) is a hybrid of *A. laevis* and *A. arborea* that has resulted in selections of similar size but with various flowering and autumn foliage attributes.

Amelanchier laevis. Courtesy of *Fine Gardening*, taken at Minnesota Landscape Arboretum.

Betula nigra Heritage (syn. *B. nigra* 'Cully').
Taken at the Cohen Garden.

Amelanchier ×grandiflora 'Autumn Brilliance' is among the most popular selections for its intense red fall color. Canada serviceberry (*A. canadensis*, syn. *A. lamarckii*, zones 3 to 8) is another species that stands out for its smaller size, 10 to 20 feet tall and also half as wide. Plants in this genus can occasionally suffer from rust, blights, and mildew, but insect and deer trouble are rare. It is best to prune serviceberries just after they flower because they produce their blooms on the previous year's growth.

Birch

Betula species and cultivars, zones 2 to 9
Spring (flowers), fall (foliage), winter (bark, stems)

Full sun to partial shade; moist, well-drained, fertile, acidic soil

While birches have handsome foliage and intriguing flowers, it is their bark that really wows audiences. From the white, peeling surface of paper birch (*Betula papyrifera* and cultivars, zones 2 to 6) to the cinnamon, exfoliating texture of river birch (*B. nigra* and cultivars, zones 4 to 9), these deer-resistant, North American native species provide extraordinary interest throughout the year. In the wild many birch trees grow to be pretty large, in excess of 50 feet tall and 30 feet wide. Their larger stature makes them a good choice for the outskirts of the garden and as the canopy for a shady border. Smaller selections such as 10- to 15-foot-tall *B. nigra* 'Little King' (zones 4 to 9) are out and about, so pay attention to plant tags at the nursery. Weeping forms such as *B. nigra* 'Summer Cascade' (zones 4 to 9) offer another level of interest.

Paper birch can be a short-lived tree. Like the rest of the genus, it sometimes suffers from winter ice damage in northern climates and is susceptible to various disease and insect problems. Choose more stress-tolerant varieties like *Betula papyrifera* Prairie Dream (syn. *B. papyrifera* 'Varen', zones 2 to 6). River birch, on the other hand, holds up better to heat and the borers and other issues that trouble many birch species. *Betula nigra* Heritage (syn. *B. nigra* 'Cully', zones 4 to 9) is regarded as one of the top performers.

Only prune birches in late summer or autumn; they are heavy bleeders when the sap is flowing in late winter and spring. In spring you can except a lovely display of dangling catkin flowers that expand up to 4 inches long. Come autumn, the 2- to 5-inch-long, diamond-shaped leaves turn excellent shades of yellow, orange, or red, depending on the species.

Redbud

Cercis species and cultivars, zones 4 to 9
Spring (flowers), spring to fall (foliage)

Full sun to partial shade; moist, well-drained, average to fertile soil

It used to be that spring was redbud's season to shine. With the introduction of new cultivars, gorgeous deep red-purple, golden yellow, or variegated foliage now provides extended interest throughout the growing season and into autumn. Even without an infusion of color, the 4-inch-long, green, heart-shaped leaves flutter beautifully in the breeze and create an excellent border backdrop. The classic bright pink to purple, half-inch-

Cercis canadensis 'Forest Pansy'.

long blossoms are still a sight to see in early spring as they cloak leafless stems. White-flowering varieties such as *Cercis canadensis* f. *alba* 'Royal White' (zones 4 to 9) are available, as is a beautiful weeping form called *C. canadensis* Lavender Twist (syn. *C. canadensis* 'Covey', zones 5 to 9).

The North American native eastern redbud (*Cercis canadensis* and cultivars, zones 4 to 9) can reach up to 30 feet tall and wide, while its cross-continental cohort, western redbud (*C. occidentalis* and cultivars, syn. *C. canadensis* var. *occidentalis*, zones 7 to 9), maintains a smaller habit that maxes out around 12 to 15 feet tall and wide. Chinese redbud (*C. chinensis* and cultivars, zones 6 to 9) puts itself almost smack dab in the middle of

Conifers Provide Year-Round Appeal

Deciduous woody plants typically offer more variety and seasonal interest in the form of flowers, colorful fall foliage, and fruit. Evergreens, especially conifers, should not be overlooked, however. Dwarf (slow-growing) conifers are an excellent choice for mixed beds, offering year-round texture and a reliable foundation for interesting color combinations. They mingle well with herbaceous companions without dominating or overwhelming a planting. They are even happy in containers.

Dwarf conifers can get to be the same size as regular selections, just maybe not in the lifetime of the gardener who planted them. They grow 6 inches or less a year. If *nana* or some other smallish-sounding moniker is in the cultivar name, you are probably looking at a dwarf variety. To be sure you are getting one, make sure the plant is dense with short internodes. Conifers can easily be mislabeled by an untrained eye; specialty nurseries can steer you in the right direction. The American Conifer Society lists good resources and provides a conifer database (which can be browsed by type) on conifersociety.org.

Typical conifer genera like *Pinus*, *Abies*, and *Picea* all offer dwarf options. All they ask for is a sunny location with moist, well-drained, slightly acidic soil. Give them a drink during periods of drought. *Taxus*, *Cephalotaxus*, *Chamaecyparis*, *Tsuga*, and *Thuja* tolerate partial shade, especially in the afternoon. Here are a few specific selections to consider for your next design scheme.

Abies balsamea '**Piccolo**' (balsam fir, zones 3 to 6)

Abies koreana '**Silberlocke**' (Korean fir, zones 4 to 8)

Cedrus deodara '**Pygmaea**' (deodar cedar, zones 6 to 9)

Cephalotaxus harringtonii '**Korean Gold**' (plum yew, zones 5 to 9)

Chamaecyparis pisifera '**Golden Mop**' (false cypress, syn. *C. pisifera* 'Filifera Nana Aurea', zones 4 to 8)

Cryptomeria japonica '**Elegans Nana**' (Japanese cedar, zones 5 to 9)

Picea orientalis '**Tom Thumb**' (oriental spruce, zones 4 to 7)

Picea pungens '**Montgomery**' (Colorado spruce, zones 3 to 7)

Pinus aristata '**Sherwood Compact**' (bristlecone pine, zones 4 to 7)

Pinus densiflora '**Low Glow**' (Japanese red pine, zones 4 to 7)

Taxus baccata '**Repandens**' (English yew, zones 5 to 8)

Thuja occidentalis '**Globosa**' (American arborvitae, zones 3 to 7)

1. *Picea pungens* 'Montgomery' (center) with a *Paeonia* cultivar (top left), *Allium* 'Globemaster' (top center), *Alchemilla mollis* (bottom center), and a *Salvia* cultivar (bottom right). Taken at the Ginsburg Garden.

2. *Abies balsamea* 'Piccolo'.

3. *Abies koreana* 'Silberlocke'. Taken at the Cohen Garden.

4. *Picea orientalis* 'Tom Thumb'.

Chionanthus virginicus.

the two, standing close to 20 feet tall and wide. The southwestern United States even has its own native redbud, *C. reniformis* (and cultivars, zones 7 to 9), which also hovers around 20 feet tall and wide. *Cercis reniformis* 'Oklahoma' is the star cultivar of this species for its wine-red flowers and glossy leaves. Eastern redbud wins the medal for the most cultivars, however, with purple-leaved 'Forest Pansy' (zones 5 to 9) and golden 'Hearts of Gold' (zones 5 to 9) at the forefront of the outstanding selections.

Redbuds can be somewhat short-lived; do not expect your adult grandchildren to enjoy the same tree you planted in your younger days. If something is going to get your redbud, it is likely to be canker or verticillium wilt. Keeping plants stress-free and healthy is the best defense. Provide them with adequate water (especially during dry spells), nutrients, and plenty of sunshine. They can be pruned in late winter to enhance their framework and shape. Redbuds are definitely worthy of a spot in the nonstop garden.

Fringe tree

Chionanthus species and cultivars, zones 3 to 9
Spring (flowers), fall (fruit)

Full sun to partial shade; moist to wet, fertile soil

Fringe tree is a wonderful little multi-stemmed tree that is widely underutilized in the landscape. In spring, clusters of white, frothy, fragrant flowers cover the branches, and the tree looks like a big, fluffy cloud dropped down from the sky. The plants are dioecious, with some producing larger male flowers and others producing female flowers that set fruit that looks like extra-large blueberries. As with most reproduction, you do need to have a male nearby to get the female to bear plentiful fruit. Our native fringe tree, *Chionanthus virginicus* (zones 3 to 9), typically grows 10 to 20 feet tall and wide with handsome, elliptic, 4- to 8-inch-long leaves. The Chinese fringe tree (*C. retusus*, zones 5 to 9) is about the same size but with slightly smaller, glossy leaves. Both species make excellent specimen plants with variable yellow fall color. Pests and diseases are so infrequent that they are not even worth mentioning. A little light pruning can be done after flowering to reveal and emphasize the multistem framework, which adds interest to the winter landscape. Cultivars are almost nonexistent. With species like these, there is really no need for "improvement."

Dogwood

Cornus species and cultivars, zones 2 to 9
Spring (flowers), summer (fruit), fall (foliage), winter (bark, stems)

Full sun to partial shade; moist, well-drained, fertile, slightly acidic soil

A lot of great woody plants come out of the genus *Cornus*, which is evidenced by the many dogwood trees and shrubs showcased in our landscapes. Because of their smallish stature, several of the tree species are the perfect choice for around patios and in beds near the house. They also rarely require pruning. Flowering dogwood (*C. florida* and cultivars, zones 5 to 9) is a striking North American native that stands around 20 feet tall and 25 feet wide—often smaller, but sometimes larger, depending on the cultivar and

Cornus kousa.

region. Because of flowering dogwood's susceptibility to numerous insects and diseases when under stress, however, *kousa* or Japanese flowering dogwood (*C. kousa* and cultivars, zones 5 to 8) is often the favored tree species. Kousa has no serious insect or disease problems and has a range of cultivar options that reach anywhere from 10 to 30 feet tall and wide.

Both *Cornus florida* and *C. kousa* produce white to pink, long-lasting flower bracts (up to 2 inches wide) in spring and red fruit that birds enjoy later in the season. They also display elliptic, 3- to 6-inch-long leaves that turn beautiful shades of bright red to deep wine in autumn. Pagoda dogwood (*C. alternifolia* and cultivars, zones 3 to 8) is another

Cornus alba 'Elegantissima'. Taken at The New York Botanical Garden.

There are also a number of dogwood shrubs to choose from. Tatarian dogwood (*Cornus alba* and cultivars, zones 2 to 7), bloodtwig dogwood (*C. sanguinea* and cultivars, zones 4 to 7), and redosier dogwood (*C. sericea* and cultivars, syn. *C. stolonifera*, zones 2 to 8) are all regarded for their gorgeous red- or yellow-stemmed cultivars that shine in winter. Tiny white flowers appear on these shrubs in 2-inch-wide clusters in late spring or early summer, and sporadically during summer. Their typical elliptic leaves have variable wine-red fall color. With a maximum size of 10 to 15 feet tall and wide, Tatarian and bloodtwig dogwoods are good choices for naturalizing, while 5- to 10-foot-tall redosier dogwood is suited for mixed borders. The colorful winter stems of all of these shrubs can also be cut and used in seasonal containers and holiday floral arrangements.

The best winter stem color appears when grown in full sun and on younger branches. Sacrificing a little height and cutting these fast growers to the ground every few years before they sprout in spring will encourage the best display. This whack-and-hack method of pruning generally revitalizes these plants. Bloodtwig tends to skate by with little trouble from canker, blight, or other diseases and insects that can impact other dogwoods. The entire genus has been known to be occasionally browsed by deer. Choose variegated shrub selections like *Cornus alba* 'Elegantissima' or trees like *C. alternifolia* Golden Shadows (syn. *C. alternifolia* 'Wstackman') for a "pop" of contrast in spring, summer, and fall.

North American native that grows to about 20 feet tall and wide with less showy, small, white puffs of clustered flowers in spring and attractive, dark red to blue fruit in summer. Cornelian cherry dogwood (*C. mas* and cultivars, zones 4 to 8) is a fairly trouble-free tree from Europe and Asia with cultivars that also range in size from 10 to 25 feet tall and wide. It produces yellow umbel flowers in early spring and red fruit in summer. Variegated selections of many of these trees are available.

Crabapple

Malus species and cultivars, zones 3 to 9
Spring (flowers), fall (foliage, fruit)

Full sun; moist, well-drained, somewhat fertile, acidic soil

Crabapples—most gardeners either love them or hate them. No doubt about it, *Malus* is a troubled genus, falling victim to diseases like fireblight, apple scab, canker, and rust. Borers and a few other insects occasionally get in on the game as well. So why are we talking about crabapples? Because if you choose disease-resistant varieties, they are phenomenal in the landscape. In spring these trees start the growing season with a bang as their branches are covered in a profusion of sweetly cupped, sometimes fragrant blossoms in shades of white, pink, or purple-red. The ovate, usually 3-inch-long leaves are pretty average all the way through summer. Then, pow—they hit you with a fantastic medley of fall color that ranges from gold to orange to red. Believe it or not, the leaves are not the best fall feature. Crabapples set colorful fruit that are as abundant as the flowers and reach the size of average marbles. Like the fall leaves, they also come in shades of yellow, orange, or red. The display is truly spectacular. Birds enjoy the sour fruit as it softens, and so do deer if they can reach it.

Because crabapples easily hybridize on their own in the wild, a great many varieties are available. Some are more or less resistant to certain diseases than others. Likewise, some diseases are more prevalent in certain areas of the country than others. Check with local nursery growers and your local Cooperative Extension office for crabapple recommen-

Malus Golden Raindrops (syn. *M.* 'Schmidtcutleaf').

dations that will work best for you. No matter which crabapple you grow, avoid planting junipers (*Juniperus* species and cultivars, zones 2 to 11). Junipers are a host for cedar apple rust, which can easily move to crabapples and regular apple trees (*Malus domestica* and cultivars, zones 4 to 8) that are in close proximity. A few beautiful crabapple selections you might consider include, from smallest to largest, *M. sargentii* (zones 4 to 8), *M.* 'Adirondack' (zones 4 to 8), *M.* 'Prairifire' (zones 4 to 8), *M.* Golden Raindrops (syn. *M.* 'Schmidtcutleaf', zones 3 to 8), and *M.* 'Donald Wyman' (zones 4 to 8). They range in size from 8 to 25 feet tall and wide and all make excellent garden focal points. Try to limit pruning to just after flowering; otherwise you will be sacrificing the following year's blooms and fruit.

Winter Wonderland

Although winter is primarily the time of year to showcase structure in the garden, this does not mean it needs to be devoid of color. Evergreens, colorful woody stems, ornamental berries, and the remnants of dry grasses and seedheads all partner together to chase away the winter blues. Flowers are not totally out of the question, either. Some woody plants, late-winter bulbs, and cool-season annuals (for more temperate climates) also strut their floral stuff in sunny spots this time of year.

Planting Plan

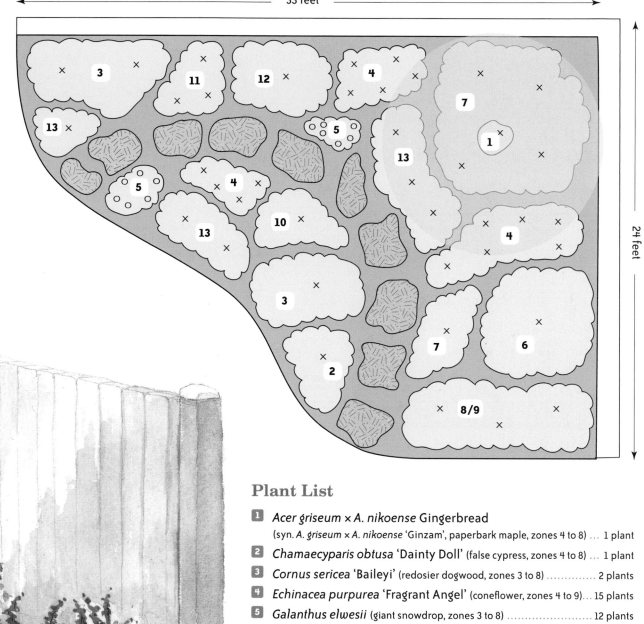

33 feet

24 feet

Plant List

1. *Acer griseum × A. nikoense* Gingerbread
   (syn. *A. griseum × A. nikoense* 'Ginzam', paperbark maple, zones 4 to 8) ... 1 plant
2. *Chamaecyparis obtusa* 'Dainty Doll' (false cypress, zones 4 to 8) ... 1 plant
3. *Cornus sericea* 'Baileyi' (redosier dogwood, zones 3 to 8) .... 2 plants
4. *Echinacea purpurea* 'Fragrant Angel' (coneflower, zones 4 to 9)... 15 plants
5. *Galanthus elwesii* (giant snowdrop, zones 3 to 8) .... 12 plants
6. *Hamamelis ×intermedia* 'Jelena' (witch hazel, zones 5 to 8) .... 1 plant
7. *Helleborus* Ivory Prince (syn. *H.* 'Walhelivor', zones 4 to 8) .... 5 plants
8. *Ilex verticillata* 'Jim Dandy' (winterberry, zones 3 to 9) .... 2 plants
9. *Ilex verticillata* 'Winter Red' (winterberry, zones 3 to 9)............... 1 plant
10. *Miscanthus sinensis* 'Morning Light' (maiden grass, zones 5 to 9) ... 1 plant
11. *Panicum amarum* 'Dewey Blue' (bitter switch grass, zones 2 to 9)... 3 plants
12. *Picea pungens* 'Baby Blueeyes' (Colorado spruce, zones 3 to 7)....... 1 plant
13. *Sedum* 'Matrona' (zones 3 to 8)... 6 plants

Cotinus coggygria 'Royal Purple'. Taken at the Cohen Garden.

SUPERB SHRUBS

A mixed border without shrubs is like dough without yeast—a flat, mushy blob that just sits there. Large and medium shrubs are a low-maintenance way to give plantings a lift. They set the stage for herbaceous plants. They can also be used to frame a view, directing focus exactly where you want it to go, like on a simple urn, bench, specimen plant, or vista that you would like to enjoy from your patio. Likewise, shrubs can block and muffle things that you would rather forget, such as the neighbor's barking dog, your trash can area, or an unsightly fence. As with trees, many shrubs are available. Take a gander at these, which all offer native options and require very little extra care.

Smokebush

Cotinus coggygria and cultivars, zones 5 to 8
Spring (flowers), spring to fall (foliage)

Full sun to partial shade; moist, well-drained, moderately fertile soil

There is something dreamy about smokebush. Maybe it is the airy essence of the 6-inch-long flowers as they mature to a green, sometimes pink or purple, haze in late spring. Perhaps it is the fresh-looking, oval leaves that can reach to almost 4 inches long. Possibly it's the billowy habit that can reach 8 to 15 feet tall and wide. Whatever it is, this shrub was made for the mixed border. Deep red-purple cultivars like 'Royal Purple' and 'Grace' offer a gorgeous color and texture that can be easily contrasted and echoed with any number of companion plants. Likewise, the golden selection Golden Spirit (syn. *Cotinus coggygria* 'Ancot') also plays quite nicely with others. The best leaf colors are produced in full sun.

Smokebushes can be troubled by verticillium wilt and a few foliar diseases, but not often. Insect and deer problems are rare. Cutting stems back to about a foot tall in spring every two or three years will deliver the richest leaf color from the purple and gold cultivars. This practice sounds scary, but it works. It does come with a price, however—no flowers and a slightly diminished size that season. Most gardeners could care less since it is the foliage they are after, and they do not want their plants to get too large anyway. Whether or not they are pruned back hard, smokebushes are really smoking when it comes to adding color and texture to the garden.

Do not be surprised if you get an impressive show in autumn. Many cultivars are known to end the gardening season with a bang, displaying brilliant yellow to orange to deep red leaves. *Cotinus* 'Flame' was chosen just for its spectacular fall extravaganza. American smoketree (*C. obovatus*, zones 4 to 8) also produces excellent fall color; it reaches 20 to 30 feet tall and almost as wide.

Fothergilla
Fothergilla species and cultivars, zones 4 to 9
Spring (flowers), fall (foliage)

Full sun to partial shade; moist to wet, well-drained, moderately fertile, acidic soil

Fothergilla is a lot like an awesome rock band just before it goes mainstream: it has a small groupie following that secretly hopes the rest of the world will not catch on. This underused genus is made up of only two species, dwarf fother-

1. *Fothergilla* ×*intermedia* 'Mount Airy'. Courtesy of *Fine Gardening*.

2. *Fothergilla* ×*intermedia* 'Blue Shadow'.

Fothergilla gardenii.

gilla (*F. gardenii*, zones 5 to 9) and large fothergilla (*F. major*, zones 4 to 8). Both are excellent native plants that basically only differ in appearance by size, as their common names suggest. Dwarf fothergilla can grow to be 2 to 6 feet tall and wide with 2-inch-long, oval leaves. Large fothergilla can reach 10 to 15 feet tall and wide, and features roundish leaves, up to 4 inches long, with slightly scalloped edges. In spring both shrubs produce fragrant, creamy white flowers that resemble 1- to 2-inch-long bottlebrushes. In autumn their leaves put on a similar display of color that is a mix of yellow, orange, and red. The effect and consistency can vary from plant to plant.

The two species are known to hybridize. One such encounter produced the popular selection *Fothergilla* ×*interme-dia* 'Mount Airy' (zones 5 to 8), a vigorous shrub that grows up to 5 feet tall, with reliable fall color and lots of spring blooms. Other notable cultivars include *F. gardenii* 'Blue Mist' and *F.* ×*intermedia* 'Blue Shadow' (zones 4 to 8), both of which feature lovely blue-green foliage. There really is no bad fothergilla. This genus has no pest or disease issues to speak of. The shrubs are at home in naturalized areas as well as highly cultivated beds. Choose dwarf fothergilla for areas with consistent moisture; it can even take somewhat wet conditions. Large fothergilla appreciates regular moisture as well but can tolerate periodic dry spells. Fothergillas rarely need pruning. If you find that your plant needs to be thinned or shaped, do it after flowering to be sure there will be blooms the following year.

Hamamelis
×*intermedia* 'Diane'.
Courtesy of *Fine Gardening*.

Witch hazel

Hamamelis species and cultivars, zones 3 to 8
Fall (foliage), winter (flowers)

Full sun to partial shade; moist, well-drained, moderately fertile, slightly acidic soil

This is without a doubt one of the best large shrub (or small tree) choices for winter interest. Just when you think the days could not get much bleaker, out comes witch hazel with an unbelievable flower display. It truly is astonishing to see a plant in bloom during the coldest months of the year. Autumn, instead of spring, is when this genus starts to rev up its engines. That is when the somewhat thick, fuzzy leaves turn from an average green to a vivid yellow, sometimes orange. The leaf shape looks very similar to large fothergilla because both genera are in the same family, Hamamelidaceae. The roundish, roughly scalloped leaves are 4 to 6 inches long—slightly larger than the fothergilla's. Sometimes witch hazels hold on to their foliage for a few months after it browns in the fall. The fragrant, wispy, yellow, orange, or red flowers are so spectacular, however, that you hardly notice this trait, although some gardeners go through the trouble of removing the crispy leaves.

Common witch hazel (*Hamamelis virginiana* and cultivars, zones 3 to 8), a North American native, is one of the first to step into the flowering spotlight, producing golden flowers on its 12- to 20-foot-tall-and-wide habit in late autumn. Next come the witch hazel hybrids (*H.* ×*intermedia* cultivars, zones 5 to 8), which can reach anywhere from 8 to 20 feet tall and wide, depending on the cultivar. The flowers open right in the dead of winter and can last up to eight to twelve weeks (no joke) when temperatures remain cold. Yellow-flowering *H. ×intermedia* 'Arnold Promise' is among prized favorites, as are orange-flowering *H. ×intermedia* 'Jelena' and red-flowering *H. ×intermedia* 'Diane'. Not long after the hybrids start doing their thing, vernal (*H. vernalis* and cultivars, zones 4 to 8), Chinese (*H. mollis* and cultivars, zones 5 to 8), and Japanese (*H. japonica* and cultivars, zones 5 to 8) witch hazels also get in on the act. They specialize in yellow flowers on their 10- to 20-foot-tall-and-wide forms. After flowering, witch hazels rest a wee bit before sending out fresh, new green leaves in spring.

Witch hazels have no serious insect or disease afflictions. While they can certainly be included in mixed plantings, they also look their best flying solo in a spot where you can enjoy them from a roasty-toasty view out a window. Otherwise you will be making tracks through snowdrifts if you want to catch a glimpse of the unique blossoms. Besides maybe occasional thinning and shaping, witch hazels require very little pruning. If you are going to make any cuts, do it in spring before the next year's flower buds form during summer. For abundant blooms, place plants where they will receive a good amount of sun. Witch hazels do not respond well to drought. Some gardeners have had success with growing them in zone 9.

Hydrangea
Hydrangea species and cultivars, zones 3 to 9
Summer to fall (flowers, foliage)

Partial shade to full sun; moist, well-drained, fertile soil

The big, billowy blooms of hydrangea make most gardeners (and nongardeners) drool. They are highly prized beacons of the summer garden and a welcome addition to mixed borders. There are lots to choose from, but the hit list includes bigleaf (*Hydrangea macrophylla* and cultivars, zones 4 to 9), panicle (*H. paniculata* and cultivars, zones 3 to 8), and oakleaf (*H. quercifolia* and cultivars, zones 5 to 9) hydrangeas. Each brings something different to the garden.

Oakleaf hydrangea has lobed leaves that resemble that of, you guessed it, an oak. Each leaf grows up to 8 inches long and has a great leathery texture. In autumn you can expect the foliage to turn gorgeous scarlet to deep wine. From summer into autumn, large (up to 12 inches long) cone-shaped flowers appear. The long-lasting blooms start out white and age to shades of pink. Pay attention to which cultivar you choose of this North American species; larger varieties will need a little space. Oakleaf hydrangeas can range in size from 3 to 10 feet tall and often slightly wider. *Hydrangea quercifolia* Snowflake (syn. *H. quercifolia* 'Brido') and *H. quercifolia* Snow Queen (syn. *H. quercifolia* 'Flemygea') are among the most popular selections for their especially large blooms.

Panicle hydrangea has flowers that are very similar to oakleaf's, only the white cones usually average around 8 inches long. The biggest differences between the two species, however, are in their leaves and forms. Panicle hydrangea has elliptic leaves that can reach up to 6 inches long. The fall color is variable with the possibility of some striking reds, but usually nothing to write home about. This hydrangea has a significant upright stature and can grow to 10 to 20 feet tall and wide, making it more like a multi-stemmed tree than a shrub. It makes a lovely specimen plant. Smaller options are also available, such as the late-flowering *Hydrangea paniculata* 'Tardiva', which only grows 8 to 12 feet tall, and *H. paniculata* 'Limelight', which tops out around 6 to 8 feet.

Bigleaf hydrangea is probably one of the most sought-after species for its blue, pink, or sometimes white blooms. Some selections produce flat, 6- to 8-inch-wide flowers called lacecaps, but it is the huge, puffy, 6- to 10-inch-round mopheads that really steal the show. This species usually grows 3 to 6 feet tall and wide (on occasion even taller and to almost twice as wide), with some dwarf, 2-foot-tall varieties also available. It has attractive, elliptic leaves up to 8 inches long, but no significant fall color. If you are more concerned about interesting foliage, white-and-green variegated options like *Hydrangea macrophylla* 'Maculata' (zones 6 to 9) are available. While many cultivars are selected for their great blue or pink flower colors, the hues you get are largely dependent on your soil. Acidic soil with a fair amount of aluminum yields blue flowers, while alkaline soil with no available aluminum results in pink blooms. Many gardeners in zone 5 and colder struggle to get most cultivars to bloom.

Hydrangea paniculata 'Tardiva'. Taken at The New York Botanical Garden.

Call of the Wild

The joy of wildlife in the garden is not to be missed. To attract hummingbirds, songbirds, and butterflies to your backyard, consider a floriferous and fruiting mix of plants that nourishes our flying friends in a sunny spot. Include a bench under the shade of a large shrub or small tree so that you can be sure to have a front-row seat. Birdhouses and birdbaths are not a bad idea, either. They give birds their own apartment and shower, and offer you a chance to add functional ornamentation to the garden.

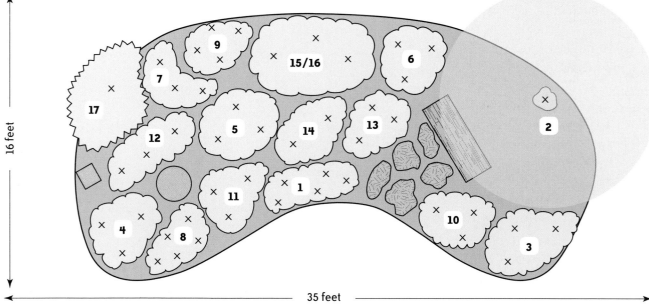

Planting Plan

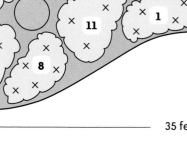

Plant List

1 *Agastache* Acapulco Salmon and Pink
(syn. *A.* 'Kiegabi', anise hyssop, zones 5 to 10) .... 5 plants

2 *Amelanchier* ×*grandiflora* 'Autumn Brilliance'
(apple serviceberry, zones 4 to 9) .... 1 plant

3 *Boltonia asteroides* var. *latisquama* Jim Crockett
(syn. *B. asteroides* var. *latisquama* 'Masbolimket',
false aster, zones 4 to 8) .... 3 plants

4 *Buddleja davidii* Lo & Behold
(syn. *B. davidii* 'Blue Chip', butterfly bush, zones 5 to 9).... 3 plants

5 *Calamagrostis* ×*acutiflora* 'Karl Foerster'
(reed grass, zones 5 to 9)...................................... 3 plants

6 *Calamagrostis brachytricha* (reed grass, zones 5 to 9) 3 plants

7 *Canna* 'Conestoga' (zones 8 to 11) .... 3 plants

8 *Dianthus barbatus* 'Heart Attack'
(sweet William, zones 3 to 8).................................. 6 plants

9 *Helenium* 'Moerheim Beauty'
(sneezeweed, zones 4 to 8)..................................... 4 plants

10 *Lantana camara* Bandana Red
(syn. *L. camara* 'Bante Reeda', zones 8 to 11) .... 3 plants

11 *Leucanthemum* ×*superbum* 'Becky'
(Shasta daisy, zones 4 to 8) .... 3 plants

12 *Monarda* 'Raspberry Wine' (bee balm, zones 4 to 9) 3 plants

13 *Phlox paniculata* 'David' (garden phlox, zones 4 to 8) 3 plants

14 *Solidago rugosa* 'Fireworks'
(goldenrod, zones 4 to 9) .... 2 plants

15 *Vaccinium* 'Blueray' (highbush blueberry, zones 4 to 7) 1 plant

16 *Vaccinium* 'Northland'
(highbush blueberry, zones 3 to 7)............................. 2 plants

17 *Viburnum opulus* var. *americanum* 'Wentworth'
(syn. *V. trilobum* 'Wentworth', American
cranberrybush viburnum, zones 2 to 7) .... 1 plant

As with all plants, incidents with insects and diseases can occur, but these problems are rare with hydrangeas. Deer can be a problem, but this genus's biggest enemies are intense winter temperatures and overeager pruners. Because many hydrangeas bloom on old wood, winter bud kill (often caused by premature bud break during unseasonably warm spells) and spring pruning will lead to no flowers. Gardeners in cooler climates should seek out cold-hardy varieties and take advantage of microclimates. They should also keep their pruners in the shed. Except for the occasional removal of a dead stem, hydrangeas rarely require pruning. If you find that your plant does need some size reduction, do it in the summer.

One way to avoid blooming problems (well, except when caused by deer) is to choose a panicle hydrangea, which blooms on new growth. Bigleaf varieties that flower on old and new growth are also becoming more common. *Hydrangea macrophylla* Endless Summer (syn. *H. macrophylla* 'Bailmer', zones 4 to 9) and *H. macrophylla* 'Penny Mac' (zones 5 to 9) are such options. By the time you finish reading this book, another fifty new cultivars will have appeared on the market. Take your time in choosing one. Some are very floppy, others stingy with their flowers, and some are just downright dogs. Watch out for the hype, and before making your choice go see the plants in action at an arboretum or a garden center with display gardens.

Holly

Ilex species and cultivars, zones 3 to 11
Fall to winter (fruit), winter to fall (foliage)

Full sun to partial shade; moist, well-drained, moderately fertile, acidic soil

The genus *Ilex* may not be known for glamorous flowers or fall color, but it is chock-full of species that provide reliable, sometimes evergreen, foliage and attractive berries. When most people hear the name holly, they think of dark green, spiny leaves on stiff, conical trees or shrubs—something along the lines of evergreen American (*I. opaca* and cultivars, zones 5 to 9) or blue (*I. ×meserveae* and cultivars, zones 5 to 7) hollies. With more than 400 species in this genus, however, more options exist beyond the usual suspects.

Winterberry (*Ilex verticillata* and cultivars, zones 3 to 9) is a prime example. One look in summer at the narrow, green, elliptic leaves up to 4 inches long and you would never guess it was a member of this clan. Come autumn you may be tipped off by the gorgeous, brilliant red, sometimes orange or yellow, berries, which last well into winter if birds do not get them. Unlike many of the more refined evergreens, this deciduous, multistemmed North American native actually likes wet soil. It is a good choice for damp or swampy sites and will form a 4- to 10-foot-tall-and-wide stand. Remember, with *Ilex* it does take two to tango, so be sure to plant a male and female in the vicinity of one another to pollinate the tiny, white female flowers in spring and get good fruit set in fall. *Ilex verticillata* 'Winter Red' is a good female to pair with

male *I. verticillata* 'Jim Dandy'. If you plan to do a mass planting, eight females to one male is a good ratio. The male will love having his harem for all that horticultural procreation.

Japanese holly (*Ilex crenata* and cultivars, zones 5 to 7) is a unique, evergreen species. Its tiny oval leaves are usually less than an inch long and look similar to boxwood. Many, many cultivars are available, all variable in form from low and spreading to tall and columnar. Japanese holly selections can range anywhere from 2 to 15 feet tall with an equally variable spread. This species is a pretty slow grower and a good choice for small gardens or tight spaces. Plants rarely need regular pruning; their dense forms look good naturally. Many cultivars, such

as fastigiate *I. crenata* 'Sky Pencil', offer extraordinary silhouettes without any help from pruners. If you do need to snip, feel free to do it at any time of year. The flowers and fruit on this species are too insignificant to notice when missing.

These plants are just the tip of the *Ilex* iceberg. If they do not float your boat, do not worry. There are lots more to explore. Just be sure to choose one that is right for your conditions. Different species can take different light, moisture, and soil types. They can also vary in pest and disease susceptibility. In general, though, hollies are not a chronically troubled bunch.

Ninebark

Physocarpus opulifolius and cultivars,
zones 3 to 8
Spring to fall (foliage), summer (flowers)

Full sun to partial shade; moist to dry, well-drained, fertile to lean soil

Not long ago ninebarks were just run-of-the-mill shrubs exhibiting average, green, 3-inch-long, maplelike leaves on stems up to 10 feet tall. Thanks to clever breeding and the introduction of deep purple 'Diablo', all that has changed. Ninebarks are now highly coveted foliage plants, used as the centerpieces in many mixed plantings. The classic, compact 'Dart's Gold' is still around, sharing its cheery early-season touch of gold. Additional selections such as Coppertina (syn. *Physocarpus opulifolius* 'Mindia') and 'Center Glow' also bring copper-toned leaves into the mix. Most ninebarks grow almost as wide as they are tall, so their upright to arching stems do a good job at screening or standing at attention in a hedgerow. Small, white to pink flowers make an appearance in early summer, the clusters looking almost like fuzzy, 2-inch-wide ping-pong balls. It is the long-lasting foliage, however, that makes this North American native great. Ninebarks suffer from no serious pest or disease problems. They are fairly fast growers that easily increase by suckering stems. They can be cut back hard to the ground in winter if they ever get to be a little too much or just need to be rejuvenated.

1. *Physocarpus opulifolius* 'Dart's Gold' (bottom left) mingles with *Physocarpus opulifolius* 'Diablo' (top center), a *Heuchera* species (bottom right), and a *Hosta* cultivar (bottom right). Taken at the Diemer Garden.

2. *Physocarpus opulifolius* 'Center Glow'.

Rhododendron

Rhododendron species and cultivars,
zones 3 to 11
Spring (flowers), winter to fall (foliage)

Partial shade; moist, well-drained, moderately
fertile, acidic soil

When most folks think of shrubs for
shade, rhododendrons often pop into
their heads. These quintessential spring-
flowering plants are a favorite among
woodland gardeners. There are well more
than 500 species, not to mention oodles
of cultivars, with azaleas also being a
part of this group. The azalea portion of
this genus typically has deciduous leaves
and can grow anywhere from 2 to 15 feet
tall with an equally variable spread. In
contrast, most rhododendrons are evergreen and can grow to the size of a small
20-foot-tall tree in areas like the Pacific
Northwest. The evergreen plants are
especially appealing for their year-round
foliage. Both azaleas and rhododendrons
produce variable-sized clusters of flowers
that come in every shade under the sun.
If you cannot find one you like, you are
not looking hard enough.

At the risk of being stoned or lynched
by *Rhododendron* enthusiasts and collectors, we have to say that a lot of the
selections in this genus kind of look alike.
Just pick a plant that appeals to you and
go from there. The main thing you want
to pay attention to, besides flower color,
is vigor. Obviously, southern gardeners
should choose heat-tolerant plants, while
northern residents will want to look for
more cold-hardy choices. There are plenty
of both to go around. Because *Rhododendron* species are easy to hybridize, breeders love playing around with this genus
and are always encouraging new selections that push past heat or cold limitations. It should not be too difficult to seek
out plants that are well-suited to your
area, which is usually what is stocked at
the local nursery or garden center. Unfortunately, breeders have not yet figured
out how to repel deer.

As you might expect from the huge
number of species, there is also a long list
potential insect pests and diseases. Native species and hybrids tend to be more
resistant to any troublemakers that may
pop up. Catawba rhododendron (*Rhododendron catawbiense* and cultivars, zones
4 to 8) is a hardy, evergreen choice that is
widely available. It prefers a cool, moist
location. Classic Dexter hybrids like *R.*
'Wheatley' (zones 5 to 8) are also a good
choice for more northerly climates. Do
not panic if the leaves roll up in winter;

Picked a Good Plant—Now What?

Because of their size and expense, trees and shrubs can be a little intimidating to plant and grow at first. They grow on the same principles of any other plant, however. Give each species the amount of light, water, and nutrients that it requires, and you are golden. Hour for hour, trees and shrubs actually require a lot less care than herbaceous plants. Here are some tips to get your trees and shrubs off to a good start.

HAVE YOUR SOIL TESTED. Before you put one plant in the ground, know what is happening in your soil. One of the great services of the Cooperative Extension System is soil testing. For a minimum fee, you can give them a soil sample and they will tell you your soil's pH, organic matter content, and nutrient levels—all important things to know when you are trying to meet the needs of your plants. Cooperative Extension offices are listed in the phonebook and online at www.csrees.usda.gov/Extension. They can tell you everything you need to know about how to prepare and submit your soil sample for testing.

DIG A GOOD HOLE. Trees and shrubs do not want to be planted too deep or too high. Like Goldilocks, they want it just right. Trees should not look like a telephone pole sticking out of the ground. If you look at them in the wild, their base is flared. When planting a new tree, find the flare and be sure that it sits an inch or two above the soil line. Likewise, plant shrubs so that the soil line in their pot or root ball is just a smidge higher (an inch) above the surface of the ground. Both trees and shrubs want a hole that is two or three times the width of their root ball or container.

Trees have a natural flare at the base. If yours looks like a telephone pole, it is planted too deep.

SKIP THE FERTILIZER. You do not need to fertilize trees or shrubs at planting time. Fertilizer in the planting hole will only encourage your woody plant to keep its roots in that vicinity. You want the roots to span out and create a good anchoring system. Amending an entire planting area or bed to improve drainage and compaction is fine because you are creating a homogeneous soil environment. You just do not want the nutrient levels directly in the hole to be drastically different from those in the surrounding area.

STAY ON TOP OF WATERING. It usually takes a year or two before a tree or shrub is really settled in. During that time, it is important to give it regular water. Thoroughly water it at planting time, and then be sure it gets a good drink a least once a week, especially during the hot summer months. To keep the water from flowing away from the root zone, build a small, 3- or 4-inch soil berm around the base of the plant at the drip line. Once the plant is established, rake the berm flat.

DO NOT FORGET TO MULCH. One of the best things you can do for your tree or shrub is to give it a good 2- to 3-inch layer of mulch. Not only does this help keep the soil moist and the roots cool, it also keeps down weeds and slowly builds the soil with organic matter. Woodchip mulch from a nursery works well, but some of the best mulch can be found in your own backyard. Shredded leaves broken down into leaf mold and good old compost made from yard waste are excellent mulches. No matter what you use, do not overdo it. Remember that flare at the base of your tree? You do not want to bury that or your shrub stems. Roots need air. Creating a mulch volcano will do nothing more than slowly suffocate your plant.

PRUNE PROBLEM BRANCHES. Unless you are pruning your tree or shrub into the shape of a bunny or lollipop, you should not have to get your pruners out very often. Most woody plants require very little pruning. The time you will want to make cuts is when you see dead, damaged, or misplaced and rubbing branches (this includes suckers). Prune the problem branch back to the next healthy lateral branch, stem, or growing point. This can be done as soon as you notice the issue. Do not leave a nub; make the cut flush and clean. Any shaping or rejuvenation pruning should be done in late winter on most plants that flower on new wood, and after flowering for those that bloom on old wood.

that is just a defense mechanism used to minimize desiccation in harsh winter environments. Exbury hybrids (*Rhododendron* cultivars, zones 5 to 9) are a large group of azaleas derived from many native crosses. Some are more heat tolerant than others. Gardeners in the South should hunt down Exbury selections like *R.* 'Admiral Semmes' (zones 6 to 9), which is part of the Confederate series, bred especially for hot climates and named in honor of heroes from the South. Also be on the lookout for deciduous options with attractive fall color, like the splendid yellow to red hues that appear in the leaves of royal azalea (*R. schlippenbachii*, zones 4 to 7).

Despite their shady reputation, rhododendrons and azaleas prefer the dappled light found at the woodland edge, not deep shade. Typically the farther north you go, the more sun they can take. One thing to be cautious with, however, is their feeding. Plants can burn from heavy fertilizer applications. The best way to feed them is with a nice mulching of organic compost each year. Do not expect to get the pruners out very often. These shrubs require very little attention beyond the removal of an occasional dead, broken, or misplaced branch.

Viburnum
Viburnum species and cultivars, zones 2 to 9
Spring (flowers), fall (foliage, fruit)

Full sun to partial shade; moist, well-drained, moderately fertile soil

Although not nearly as big as *Rhododendron*, *Viburnum* is another genus with an exhaustive list of species (more than 100) with lots of cultivars. This group has a good reputation for producing showy flowers, fruit, and fall leaf color. The white flowers appear in spring and vary in form from flat corymbs to fluffy panicles, somewhat reminiscent of lacecap and mophead hydrangea blooms, only a quarter to half the size. Depending on the variety, viburnums can grow 3 to 15 feet tall with a width that comes pretty close to the height. The leaves can be ovate to rounded to maplelike with smooth or toothed edges. They usually span 3 to 5 inches long and turn lovely shades of yellow, orange, or red in fall. Bright red berries are another common autumn feature and are enjoyed by birds. Some species host a cosmic display of fruit color. Smooth witherod (*V. nudum* and cultivars, zones 3 to 9) produces berries that start out pale pink, intensify to the shade of a pink gumball, and finally mature to blue. The cultivars 'Winterthur' and 'Earthshade' trump that by adding beautiful red fall leaves to the scene.

It is difficult to find a bad viburnum. As long as they are given regular moisture, they are a pretty easygoing brood. Until viburnum leaf beetle came over from Europe, these plants lived largely untroubled by any serious pests or diseases. So far this insect problem seems

to be concentrated in the northeastern United States. Unfortunately, it looks like the North American native species, such as nannyberry (*Viburnum lentago*, zones 2 to 7) and arrowwood (*V. dentatum* and cultivars, zones 4 to 9), are most at risk. The good news is that beneficial insects like lady beetles are helping out by feeding on viburnum leaf beetle larva.

Viburnums require very little pruning. Removing a few old stems every few years in late winter will keep them fresh and productive. Viburnums are a great choice for the mixed border and can also be used to create a screening hedge, in mass plantings, or as a foundation focal point. Some species tolerate more shade than others. Mapleleaf viburnum (*Viburnum acerifolium* and cultivars, zones 3 to 9) is a good choice for shady locations. American cranberrybush viburnum (*V. opulus* var. *americanum* and cultivars, syn. *V. trilobum*, zones 2 to 7) is a great pick for partially shaded sites.

1. *Viburnum opulus* 'Compactum'.

2. *Viburnum nudum* 'Earthshade'.

4 Perennials

Along with trees and shrubs, perennials are part of the core crew of reliable plants for the nonstop garden. Perennials are great because they come back year after year, but some are more trouble than they are worth—with brief showmanship, high care requirements, or lots of pest and disease issues.

Although perennials are known for their flowers, many stand out even when not in bloom. Clockwise from top: *Polygonatum odoratum* 'Variegatum', *Hosta* 'Aphrodite', *Alchemilla mollis*, and a *Helleborus* cultivar. Taken at The New York Botanical Garden.

The best perennials have a long season of bloom, great foliage, few pests and diseases, and are fairly self-sustaining. The good news is that lots of plants offer these attributes. As with all things gardening, however, choices are largely regionally dependent. What works best in Georgia will not always be the right choice for gardeners in Minnesota, and vice versa. Looking at a plant's hardiness zone range gives you a good jumping-off point.

Of course, light exposure is another important consideration. Most mixed borders, depending on the size of the trees and shrubs, have both sunny and shady spots. That is the best of all possible worlds, giving you lots of plants to choose from. Keep in mind that full sun is considered at least six hours of direct sunlight. When it comes to perennials, you can often get away with a little light or partial shade. Afternoon sun is quite strong, however, so three to four hours of afternoon sun may give full-sun plants a sufficient tan. Conversely, shade plants can handle—and often welcome—morning sun, but afternoon sun is a big no-no. With that in mind, the following sun and shade perennials are good plants to consider. Have fun exploring your options.

SUN-LOVING SHOWSTOPPERS

Asking a gardener to choose their favorite perennial is like asking a kid to pick their favorite candy. It depends on your mood, the time of year, and maybe which way the breeze is blowing. Perennials are all good in their own way. Narrowing down plants for sun is especially difficult because there are so many great options. The best way to go about it is to start with seasonality. Choose a mix of perennials that will peak with blooms at different times throughout the year and still look pretty good when the flowers are out for the count. Flower and leaf color are often the next characteristics to look for, but do not forget to also consider plant and leaf size. A variable mix of both will keep beds and borders from appearing flat and prevent plants from getting lost in the crowd. Echoing some of these characteristics also helps to gel plantings together. Striking a balance between contrast and repetition is a key component to good design.

Anise hyssop

Agastache species and cultivars, zones 4 to 11
Summer (flowers)

Conditions: Full sun; moderately moist, well-drained, average soil

Anise hyssop, also known as hummingbird mint, is a top pick for butterfly and hummingbird gardens. Add that to its low-maintenance demeanor, deer and rabbit resistance, long bloom time, and sturdy upright stems, and you will not want to be without it. Although it is in the mint family (those square stems are a giveaway), this genus has a well-behaved, clump-forming habit that really holds up in the midrange of the mixed border. The licorice-scented foliage is gray-green to silvery, and fuzzy as it attractively fills the base of the plant before continuing sporadically up the stem. The new leaves appear as soon as the soil warms, and plants grow to full size by early summer.

Depending on the cultivar, anise hyssops usually reach 12 to 36 inches tall with an equal spread. Throughout summer, tiny-throated flowers in shades of purple, pink, or orange form clusters up to the ends of the stems, creating a mass of 5-inch-long flower spikes. *Agastache* 'Blue Fortune' (zones 5 to 9) is a great choice with lavender-blue flowers, while *A.* 'Black Adder' (zones 6 to 9) is a long-blooming look-alike for early-flowering *Salvia nemorosa* 'Caradonna' (zones 4 to 8). *Agastache rupestris* cultivars (zones 5 to 8) are easy-care plants with bushier habits and flowers that appear in warm desert clay tones. *Agastache rugosa* 'Golden Jubilee' (zones 5 to 9) offers gold foliage. These plants require very little care, aside from cutting back spent foliage and stems at the end of the gardening season.

Bluestar

Amsonia species and cultivars, zones 3 to 10
Spring (flowers), fall (foliage)

Full sun to partial shade; moist, well-drained, average soil

Bluestars are wonderful multiseason perennials. In late spring the glossy, oval, medium green leaves of common bluestar (*Amsonia tabernaemontana*, zones 3 to 9) are topped with a crown of blue, half-inch, star-shaped flowers that form a landing pad for butterflies. Their flowers last for about a month in late spring, but at 3 feet tall and wide, these tough, bushy plants can serve as a low hedge if you shear them after the blooms are finished. Come fall, common bluestar steps back into the spotlight. This North American native is considered among the best for perennial fall foliage. The whole plant

Agastache 'Blue Fortune'. Taken at the Fellerman Garden.

turns a true gold that glows in the moonlight when the weather cools down, as shrubs and trees turn contrasting shades of red and orange. This is a fantastic effect to brighten ho-hum parking areas, retaining walls, or other exposed sites where grasses alone just are not enough. Threadleaf or Hubricht's bluestar (*A. hubrichtii*, zones 5 to 9) has narrow leaves and paler blue flowers in spring but the same striking fall color. Both species form mounds that vary in size from 1 to 3 feet tall and wide. *Amsonia* 'Blue Ice' (zones 4 to 9) is a compact hybrid that hovers around 12 to 18 inches tall. Bluestars are easygoing and disease and insect resistant. They make great filler plants for the midborder and are a good choice for sustainable designs.

Artemisia

Artemisia species and cultivars, zones 3 to 9
Spring to fall (foliage)

Full sun to partial shade; moderately dry, well-drained, lean soil

Believe it or not, too many flowers can muddy up a design. Blooms need contrast and backdrops to make them "pop." *Artemisia* is a genus filled with a supporting cast of players that offer silvery, fine-textured leaves that help the stars stand out. Unfortunately saddled with horrible common names like wormwood and mugwort, artemisias are masters at filling in gaps in the midborder and along the edges of walkways with reliable soft, feathery foliage that lasts from spring until fall's first hard frost. With more than 200 species ranging from 4 to 24 inches, this genus is bound to have some-

Amsonia hubrichtii.

thing that works for your sunny areas. *Artemisia* 'Powis Castle' (zones 6 to 9) has ferny leaves, is often treated like an annual, and is a good choice for containers. *Artemisia ludoviciana* 'Valerie Finnis' (zones 4 to 9) has strappy leaves and fits in well in beds and borders. Both plants can reach up to 2 feet tall and wide.

When flower buds appear in early summer, artemisias can be sheared to keep them looking full. Gardeners with monochromatic planting themes will find artemisias especially useful in creating needed color and textural breaks. No worries about deer or rabbits here: the biggest foe of these plants is poor drainage, which leads to rot. Stems can be cut back hard to 2 inches tall once plants have started to awaken in spring; just be sure to leave some of the woody trunk, much as you would with other woody herbs. Plants with an herbaceous base should be divided every three to five years when the centers become too dense and start to die out. Watch out for aggressive species like *Artemisia vulgaris* (zones 3 to 9) and its cultivars, which are out to take over the world. Of course, if your goal is to harvest your artemisia as an herbal plant, let it go wild. Artemisias are not the best choice for southern climates because they melt out (rot) in the heat and humidity. Gardeners in zone 7 and higher should test-drive one or two before fully committing.

Artemisia 'Powis Castle' (bottom) combined with *Echinacea purpurea* 'White Swan' (left of center), *Lilium* 'Casa Blanca' (top center), a *Nicotiana* cultivar (center), *Phlox paniculata* 'David' (right of center), and a *Scaevola aemula* cultivar (bottom right). Taken at the Leva Garden.

Wild indigo

Baptisia species and cultivars, zones 3 to 9
Spring (flowers), summer to fall (foliage, seedpods)

Full sun; well-drained, sandy to average soil

Every garden should have at least one wild indigo. This group of underused North American perennials, also called false indigo, boasts an impressive list of desirable attributes. Not only do they display loads of flowers in late spring, but they also feature attractive leaves and seedpods and are drought tolerant, deer resistant, long-lived, and easy to grow. The pealike flowers range in color from white to yellow to blue and grow to be 12 to 20 inches long. Wild indigos are good substitutes for lupines (*Lupinus* species and cultivars, zones 4 to 10) because they blow them out of the water with their unpretentious attitude. Used as a source for dye in early American history, these plants produce a 2- to 5-foot-tall collection of sturdy, up to half-inch-thick, stems that form a clump that is almost equally as wide.

Wild indigo can be treated like a small, rounded shrub in a border. It may take a little time for it to reach its full glory, but your patience will most certainly be rewarded. After the flowers fade, the unusual, blue-green, round, compound leaves create a striking backdrop for later bloomers. Resist the impulse to deadhead the flowers or you will miss out on the fantastic seedpods, which make a lovely rattle in the late summer breeze. Plants

Baptisia 'Purple Smoke'.

may require staking if placed in a rich, partly shaded site; they are meant for hot, sunny, lean beds. They resent transplanting. In some areas, voles may damage roots, but typically you can expect a completely pest- and disease-free performance. Classic *Baptisia* 'Purple Smoke' (zones 4 to 9) has great, muted purple flowers, while *B.* ×*varicolor* 'Twilite' (Prairieblues series, zones 4 to 8) has excellent, bicolored purple and yellow blooms. Plenty of solid yellow forms are also available, such as *B. sphaerocarpa* 'Screamin' Yellow' (zones 5 to 9).

Grasses and Ferns are First-Rate Fillers

Textural fillers are a great way to thread reliable, fine contrast through the garden. This can be done with ornamental grasses in sun or ferns in shade. Of course, some grasses and ferns can take a bit more shade or sun as long as adequate moisture is provided. If you choose the best ones for your site, you will find these tireless workhorses supplying foliar interest for most of the year. When left standing, grasses are superb for winter interest. Once established, grasses and ferns require little extra care aside from an annual removal of spent stems in early spring and occasional division to rejuvenate plants. Some plants, like maiden grass, can be more vigorous than others in certain locations. Always be sure to check your local invasive listings before bringing a new plant on board.

Great grasses

***Carex* species and cultivars** (sedge, zones 3 to 10, partial shade)

***Festuca* species and cultivars** (fescue, zones 3 to 8, full sun)

***Hakonechloa macra* and cultivars** (Japanese forest grass, zones 5 to 9, partial to full shade)

***Miscanthus sinensis* and cultivars** (maiden grass, zones 5 to 9, full sun)

***Panicum virgatum* and cultivars** (switch grass, zones 4 to 9, full sun)

***Pennisetum* species and cultivars** (fountain grass, zones 5 to 11, full sun)

***Schizachyrium scoparium* and cultivars** (little blue stem, zones 3 to 9, full sun)

Fantastic ferns

***Adiantum* species and cultivars** (maidenhair fern, zones 3 to 10, partial to full shade)

***Athyrium* species and cultivars** (lady fern, zones 3 to 9, partial to full shade)

***Dryopteris* species and cultivars** (wood fern, zones 3 to 9, partial to full shade)

***Nephrolepis* species and cultivars** (Boston fern, zones 9 to 11, partial shade)

***Osmunda* species and cultivars** (flowering fern, zones 3 to 9, partial shade to full sun)

***Polypodium* species and cultivars** (polypody, zones 3 to 11, partial shade to full sun)

***Polystichum* species and cultivars** (shield fern, zones 3 to 9, partial shade)

1. *Carex elata* 'Aurea'.

2. *Festuca* 'Siskiyou Blue'.

3. *Miscanthus sinensis* 'Morning Light'.
Taken at The New York Botanical Garden.

4. *Athyrium* 'Branford Beauty'.

5. *Dryopteris carthusiana* (top) and *D. erythrosora* (bottom). Taken at The New York Botanical Garden.

6. *Osmunda cinnamomea*.

Echinacea purpurea 'Fragrant Angel'.

Coneflower

Echinacea species and cultivars, zones 3 to 9
Summer (flowers), fall to winter (seedheads)

Full sun; moist, well-drained, average soil

It is an understatement to say that breeders have been having fun with coneflowers. There are lots to choose from these days. The traditional, purple, daisylike flowers with downward-pointing petals are no longer the main event. Yellow, orange, pink, green, and white blooms are available in various sizes and forms, including bizarre-looking doubles. On top of that, some are fragrant, dwarf, variegated, or produce multiple flowers on each stem.

Coneflowers have sturdy, upright stems and can range in size from 1 to 5 feet tall with a 2- to 3-foot-wide spread. All still have bristly, medium green leaves that make a solid background for the flowers. Whether you are using the 5-foot-tall types in the back of the border or the foot-tall dwarfs in front, the wildlife attraction is the same. If butterflies and goldfinches are a must-have for your garden, coneflowers should probably be on your shopping list, since the flowers and seedheads attract these critters. They are simple to grow in almost any sunny garden and are easy to divide and share after a few years. The new cultivars are so profuse and constantly evolving that there is no way to keep an up-to-date tally. The Big Sky series contains lots of excellent choices in a wide range of colors. *Echinacea purpurea* 'Fragrant Angel' (zones 4 to 9) is a nice, fragrant, white selection. The list goes on and on—have fun selecting your favorite.

Joe-Pye weed

Eupatorium species and cultivars, zones 3 to 10
Summer to fall (flowers)

Full sun to partial shade; wet to moist, average
soil

Looking for another North American native that can hold down the back of the border and still get cut back at the end of the season for a straightforward border cleanup? Joe-Pye weed, sometimes called boneset, is the plant for you. *Eupatorium maculatum* 'Gateway' (zones 4 to 8) has become a regular player in the group and features whorled, serrate, dark, rough foliage on 6-foot stalks. Its 4-foot-wide clumps stay clean of pests and diseases all season. By the end of July through September, the stems are topped with huge, dusky rose, domed flowers that attract all the butterflies you could possibly want. If you have a location that tends to stay extra wet, all the better; in fact Joe-Pye weed is happier yet along a creek where it can grow even taller. Because this perennial prefers cool weather or a valley, keeping the roots cool and wet fools it into being its biggest and best.

If your garden is small and you just can't squeeze one in, try one of the more petite selections like *Eupatorium dubium*

Eupatorium dubium 'Little Joe' (right) and *Perovskia atriplicifolia* (left). Courtesy of *Fine Gardening*, taken at the Chadwick Arboretum and Learning Gardens.

Geranium Rozanne (syn. *G.* 'Gerwat', bottom) with *Hakonechloa macra* 'Albovariegata' (top). Taken at The New York Botanical Garden.

'Little Joe' (zones 4 to 8) or *E. dubium* 'Baby Joe' (zones 4 to 8), which stand at 4 feet tall and just under 3 feet tall, respectively. Big gardens can enjoy the smaller Joes, too. They are great in the midborder and combine well with fall-blooming asters (*Symphyotrichum* species and cultivars, syn. *Aster*, zones 3 to 9). *Eupatorium* species also work in a medicinal theme garden and have a long history of uses. The seeds of Joe-Pye weeds can be troublesome, so deadhead your plant if you need to keep it contained. Also avoid transplanting specimens from drainage ditches or the roadside, unless you want a 12-foot monster to swallow up your garden.

Hardy geranium

Geranium species and cultivars, zones 3 to 9
Spring to summer (flowers), spring to fall (foliage)

Full sun to partial shade; moist, well-drained, average soil

About 16 *Geranium* species out of 250 are commonly used in gardens and are adaptable to both rock and shade gardens. These amazing plants have small, soft, palm-shaped, fuzzy leaves (some more deeply cut than others) that sprout from thin stems. Geraniums, also often referred to as cranesbills, typically form 1- to 2-foot-tall mounds or sprawl as a low ground cover. The buttercup-shaped flowers have five petals in pastel shades of pink, blue, lilac, and white. Some blooms exhibit dark venation while others have a double form. Depending on the variety, the 1-inch-round flowers are either scattered among the foliage or held upright on attractive stems and look like a bouquet hovering above the perfectly round mound of leaves.

Geranium Rozanne (syn. *G.* 'Gerwat', zones 5 to 8) is a great long-season bloomer that takes on a nice reddish brown color at the onset of cooler autumn temperatures. Leaf color on some selections is not limited to fall. Plants can display bronze tones or dark splashy markings, like those featured on *G. phaeum* var. *phaeum* 'Samobor' (zones 4 to 7) throughout the gardening season. With good air circulation and drainage, geraniums tend to be resistant to powdery mildew. Pests rarely trouble them. North American native *G. maculatum* (zones 3 to 8) has a broad hardiness range, tolerates shade, and covers the ground with pink flowers in spring. The cultivar 'Espresso' has handsome, dark mocha foliage.

Iris

Iris species and cultivars, zones 3 to 10
Spring to fall (flowers)

Full sun to partial shade; wet to moist, average soil

Irises have been a fixture in cultivated gardens for ages, serving as classic companions to roses (*Rosa* species and cultivars, zones 2 to 11). A wide variety are available, with every flower color you could imagine. Although iris devotees have done their best to organize this genus by creating numerous categories, it can seem daunting to select a variety for your garden. Start by finding a category that matches your conditions, and go from there.

Iris contains a wide range of species adaptable to different settings.

The 6-inch-tall, North American native crested iris (*I. cristata* and cultivars, zones 3 to 8) is drought tolerant and can be found nestled among boulders and in woodlands. Yellow flag iris (*I. pseudacorus* and cultivars, zones 5 to 9) is a hefty, 4-foot-tall species from Europe that loves water, but it has become a problematic weed in many state waterways, so check your state invasive lists before going down that path. Bearded German iris (*I. germanica* and cultivars, zones 3 to 10) works well in spots with full sun to partial shade and average, moist yet well-draining soil. It ranges in size from 1 to 3 feet tall but is sometimes troubled by iris borers. Siberian iris (*I. sibirica* and cultivars, zones 3 to 9), a beardless species, grows to about the same maximum height but is less susceptible to borers and can flourish in soggier sites.

Iris 'Immortality'. Courtesy of Sunny Border Nurseries.

A Walk on the Dark Side

Few things are more refreshing than a walk through a woodland area on a hot summer day. With a protective canopy of tall trees above, these shady retreats may not always be as showy as sunny borders, but they usually offer some interesting scenes. Woodland gardens follow Mother Nature's lead with a layering of understory trees or shrubs and a mix of herbaceous plants at your feet. Lots of interesting, seasonal vignettes are sure to be found in shady nooks and crannies throughout the year. If you play your cards right, you can even expand your shady theme to include all North American natives, like the design shown here.

Planting Plan

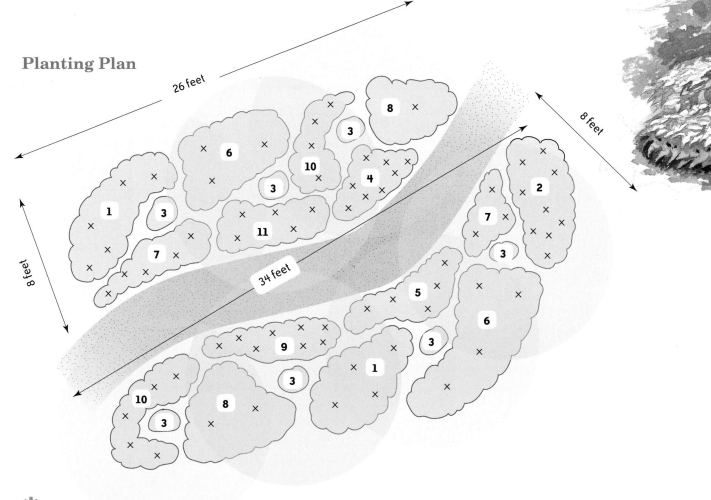

Plant List

1. *Actaea racemosa* (snakeroot, zones 3 to 8) .... 9 plants
2. *Aquilegia canadensis* (Canadian columbine, zones 3 to 8) .... 9 plants
3. *Betula nigra* Heritage (syn. *B. nigra* 'Cully', river birch, zones 4 to 9) .... 7 plants
4. *Carex appalachica* (Appalachian sedge, zones 3 to 8).. 8 plants
5. *Dryopteris marginalis* (eastern wood fern, zones 3 to 8)............................... 5 plants
6. *Fothergilla ×intermedia* 'Blue Shadow' (zones 4 to 8) .... 7 plants

7. *Heuchera* 'Brownies' (coral bells, zones 4 to 9) .... 8 plants
8. *Hydrangea quercifolia* Snowflake (syn. *H. quercifolia* 'Brido', oakleaf hydrangea, zones 5 to 9) .... 3 plants
9. *Iris cristata* 'Powder Blue Giant' (crested iris, zones 3 to 8).. 8 plants
10. *Pycnanthemum muticum* (mountain mint, zones 4 to 8) .... 9 plants
11. *Symphyotrichum cordifolius* 'Avondale' (syn. *Aster cordifolius* 'Avondale', wood aster, zones 3 to 8)............. 5 plants

Rudbeckia subtomentosa 'Henry Eilers' (center) with *Pennisetum alopecuroides* 'Hameln' (bottom right). Taken at Terra Nova Nurseries.

If you are looking for a starter iris, consider *Iris* 'Immortality' (zones 3 to 9). It is a great, fairly drought-tolerant selection that features intensely fragrant, pure white, bearded blooms that stand on 29-inch-tall stems in late spring and again in late summer or autumn. Its lovely, blue-green, swordlike foliage is not troubled by deer. Variegated sweet iris (*I. pallida* 'Argentea Variegata', zones 4 to 9) is another excellent, slightly taller choice, not for its average lavender-blue flowers but for its white-streaked blue-green leaves. It likes mostly sunny sites with good drainage.

Black-eyed Susan
Rudbeckia species and cultivars, zones 3 to 10
Summer (flowers)

Full sun to partial shade; moist, well-drained, average soil

There may be no wildflower more iconic in the United States than black-eyed Susan. Our native genus *Rudbeckia* is well known to nongardeners and gardeners alike, especially those who were around in the 1960s when the daisylike blooms became a pop culture graphic symbolizing flower power. Although some *Rudbeckia* species also commonly go by the names brown-eyed Susan or coneflower, these summertime charmers have fairly similar blooms with dark centers circled by symmetrical, yellow petals. Upright, 2- to 6-foot-tall stems hold up these floral parasols, which act as butterfly beacons until fall when they turn into a seed buffet for goldfinches. The hairy, dark green, lance-shaped, basal leaves are not much to look at, with the exception of the huge leaves of *R. maxima* (zones 5 to

9), which are blue-green and up to 2 feet long as they grow from 5- to 8-foot-tall stems. *Rudbeckia fulgida* var. *sullivantii* 'Goldsturm' (zones 3 to 9) is probably the most widely grown black-eyed Susan. At 3 feet tall and 2 feet wide, it is a gardening staple of the mixed border. *Rudbeckia subtomentosa* 'Henry Eilers' (zones 4 to 8) is a unique selection with quilled flower petals that stand on 3- to 5-foot-tall stems. Black-eyed Susans are largely trouble free. If you are not concerned with the seedheads, deadheading will prolong the bloom period. Plants placed in partial shade can be a little floppy.

Sage
Salvia species and cultivars, zones 4 to 11
Summer (flowers)

Full sun; moist, well-drained, moderately fertile to average soil

Without a doubt, there seems to be an endless supply of sages. The genus *Salvia* is chock-full of species native to almost every continent. While we grow many of the plants from south of the border as annuals, we also have a large number of hardy perennial options. Sages vary in size from 1 to 5 feet tall and up to equally as wide. They produce spikes covered with colorful, tubular flowers in shades of purple, blue, red, pink, and white, and serve up sweet nectar that brings in loads of butterflies and hummingbirds. The foliage is typically rough, a little crinkled, mostly basal, and often scented in some way when crushed. The purple-flowering selections *S. nemorosa* Marcus (syn. *S. nemorosa* 'Haeumanarc', zones 4 to 8) at 10 inches tall, *S. nemorosa* 'Caradonna' (zones 4 to 8) at 24 inches tall, and

Salvia nemorosa 'Lubecca' (top) with a *Nigella* species (left) and *Silene armeria* (bottom right). Courtesy of *Fine Gardening*, taken at Chanticleer Garden.

S. nemorosa 'Lubecca' (zones 4 to 8) at 30 inches tall are popular hardy choices, as are pink-flowering *S. nemorosa* 'Sensation Rose' (zones 4 to 8) at 14 inches tall and *S. nemorosa* 'Pink Friesland' (zones 4 to 8) at 12 inches tall. Their dense flowers appear in early summer to midsummer. Some of the less cold hardy types can be much taller, such as 4-foot-tall *S.* 'Indigo Spires' (zones 7 to 11).

These varieties are certainly just the tip of the iceberg. You can find low-growing plants like the herb common sage (*Salvia officinalis* and cultivars, zones 4 to 8) for bed edges or taller beauties like late-flowering *S. transsylvanica* (zones 4 to 7) for the mixed border. What they all have in common is the need for deadheading; if left alone, they will not live up to their reputations as long bloomers. If you are in a colder climate you may find that the very late blooming salvias do not flower before the first frost. There are a great number of sages, however, and it should not be difficult to find one that is just right for your setting.

Sedum

Sedum species and cultivars, zones 3 to 11
Spring to fall (foliage), summer to fall (flowers), fall to winter (seedheads)

Full sun to partial shade; moderately moist, well-drained, average to lean soil

Once relegated to the obscure cactus garden as nonprickly companions, sedums (or stonecrops) have come into their own as standard garden stalwarts. This undemanding, easy-care group works well in the mixed border or can be featured in monoculture designs in containers or along roadways, walls, roofs, or any

other sustaining crevice. Even though sedums have shallow roots and low-water needs, they put on a good show and are anything but boring. *Sedum* Autumn Joy (syn. *S.* 'Herbstfreude', zones 3 to 8) has been attracting butterflies and gardeners for years with its red flowers that appear from late summer through fall atop 2-foot-tall stems covered with handsome, round, fleshy leaves. *Sedum* 'Autumn Fire' (zones 3 to 9) is a compact, more upright version, while *S.* 'Matrona' (zones 3 to 8) is a very similar variety with reddish stems and reddish-tinged leaves.

Some plants can appear a little floppy, but this can easily be remedied by pinching stem tips back at their first set of leaves in late spring or early summer to encourage bushier growth. Other *Sedum* species and cultivars offer a wide range of sizes (from 2 to 24 inches tall) and foliage colors, and the foliage can be even more interesting than the flowers. Deep purple, yellow, gray, and variegated leaves make plantings stand out and combine well with other perennials, annuals, and woody plants—pretty much any plant that likes similar conditions. *Sedum rupestre* 'Angelina' (zones 6 to 9) is a great ground cover with golden, needlelike leaves; it also works well spilling over the edge of containers. The North American native *S. ternatum* (zones 3 to 8) is the most tolerant of shady, moist sites, where it forms a mat of white spring flowers while other mat-forming, evergreen types are lighting up sunny rock and trough gardens. Many gardeners wait until early spring to cut dead winter stems back, as the stems and dried flower heads provide winter interest. Sedums can also be easily propagated from cuttings if you are looking to increase your collection. The

1. *Sedum* 'Matrona' (right) with *Schizachyrium scoparium* (top left) and *Euphorbia hypericifolia* Diamond Frost (syn. *E. hypericifolia* 'Inneuphe', bottom left). Taken at the Benner Garden.

2. *Symphyotrichum oblongifolius* 'Raydon's Favorite'.

only major strike against them is that they can sometimes be browsed by deer.

Aster

Symphyotrichum species and cultivars (syn. *Aster*), zones 3 to 9
Summer to fall (flowers)

Full sun to partial shade; moist, well-drained, average soil

This group of plants has been recategorized from the genus *Aster* to *Symphyotrichum*. Do not let any new plant tags fool you, though: these are still good old asters. If you want late-summer and fall flowers, these are the perennials for you. A long list of North American native and exotic species and cultivars are available, all of which provide blooms in shades of white, pink, blue, or purple. Because sizes run the gamut from 6 inches to 8 feet tall, there is no reason not to tuck them into even the smallest garden. In larger spaces they can be used in a mass where naturalized spring bulbs also reside to extend the bloom season—making lots of butterflies and bees happy in the process. Small, medium green leaves line the plants' wiry stems and are typically of little interest other than to support the bouquets of daisylike flowers, which are also nice in a vase. One exception is *S. lateriflorus* 'Lady in Black' (zones 4 to 8) with 3-foot-tall, dark purple stems and purple-tinged foliage accompanied by tiny, pinkish white flowers.

Other noteworthy asters include 3-foot-tall *Symphyotrichum* ×*frikartii* 'Mönch' (zones 5 to 8) with large, blue flowers;

Gaillardia 'Oranges and Lemons' (center) and *Stachys byzantina* 'Big Ears' (syn. *S. byzantina* 'Countess Helen von Stein', bottom) contrast with *Panicum virgatum* 'Shenandoah' (top). Taken at Chanticleer Garden.

We are often fixated on big, bold, showy plants, but let's not forget about utilitarian ground covers. These plants offer a finished appearance and provide a low-maintenance option for large, fairly neglected areas that we still want to look good. Expanses of mulch are not attractive and eventually attract weeds. Giant mulch piles look like the last job on *The Sopranos* and make you wonder who is buried there. Ground covers provide interesting foliage and a foundation for textural contrast with other plants. They also suppress weeds, which is always a good thing.

As you begin to choose ground covers, do not forget to consider how vigorous you want these plants to be. Clump-forming plants like blanket flower or hosta may be the best option for smaller areas where other perennial neighbors will reside, while bugleweed is a great choice for big spaces that you want to cover quickly and where you are not concerned about botanical manners.

Ajuga reptans **and cultivars** (bugleweed, zones 3 to 9, full sun to full shade)

Bergenia **species and cultivars** (pigsqueak, zones 3 to 9, partial shade to full sun)

Epimedium **species and cultivars** (barrenwort, zones 4 to 9, partial to full shade)

Euphorbia **species and cultivars** (spurge, zones 4 to 11, full sun to partial shade)

Gaillardia **species and cultivars** (blanket flower, zones 3 to 9, full sun)

Hemerocallis **species and cultivars** (daylily, zones 3 to 10, full sun to partial shade)

Lamium **species and cultivars** (dead nettle, zones 4 to 8, full to partial shade)

Liriope muscari **and cultivars** (lilyturf, zones 6 to 10, partial to full shade)

Nepeta **species and cultivars** (catmint, zones 3 to 9, full sun)

Stachys byzantina **and cultivars** (lamb's ears, zones 4 to 8, full sun)

1. *Bergenia* 'Solar Flare' (center) and *Heuchera* 'Amethyst Mist' (bottom and right).

2. *Euphorbia palustris*.

3. *Hemerocallis* 'Happy Returns'.

4. *Lamium maculatum* 'Anne Greenaway'.

2-foot-tall *S. cordifolius* 'Avondale' (zones 3 to 8) with medium, blue flowers; 3-foot-tall *S. oblongifolius* 'Raydon's Favorite' (zones 3 to 8) with medium, purple flowers; and 16-inch-tall *S.* 'Wood's Pink' (zones 5 to 8) with clear pink flowers. Plants typically look their best if divided every couple of years. Taller plants can be cut back by half in early summer to encourage more compact, bushy plants. Some asters will get rust, powdery mildew, or wilt. Seek out resistant selections if you live an area where these diseases are a problem. Beyond that, asters are easy to grow. Pick at least one to boost the late-summer to fall color in your garden from plain to spectacular.

SHADY CHARACTERS

While shade plants do offer some flowers, foliage is the dominant characteristic to look for in darker locations. Choosing a mix of greens, rich colors, and variegated forms will give you the most interest. For the greatest impact, plant your perennials in larger groups or sweeps. Anything less than groups of three will leave you with a chaotic one-of-this-and-one-of-that effect. Try not to plant your groupings in a straight line. Instead give them a random configuration using odd numbers; this makes plantings look more naturalistic.

Snakeroot

Actaea and cultivars, zones 3 to 9
Spring to fall (foliage), summer to fall (flowers)

Partial to full shade; moist, fertile soil

Formerly designated under *Cimicifuga*, this fantastic group of shade perennials should be in every cool woodland garden for a couple of reasons. First, the foliage is beautiful. The finely cut leaves unfurl in shades from dark green to deep purple, almost black. Plants grow up to 3 to 4 feet tall and form rounded clumps that can be equally as wide. The leaves are somewhat reminiscent of Japanese maples (*Acer palmatum* and cultivars, zones 5 to 8) and astilbes (*Astilbe* species and cultivars, zones 4 to 9) and make an interesting contrast to the usual broad-leaved shade plants, like hostas (*Hosta* species and cultivars, zones 3 to 9).

The second notable attribute is the flowers. Often considered better than the leaves, the long, white spires reach up to 2 feet long and appear for up to four weeks in late summer. They produce an intoxicating vanilla fragrance. You do not have to stick your nose right in a flower and battle the bees to get a whiff, either. A gentle breeze will generously share the wonderful scent. The seedpods can also be an attractive addition to cut-flower bouquets. The North American native *Actaea racemosa* (zones 3 to 8) is a good naturalizer but can also be encouraged to spread by root division in spring. *Actaea simplex* 'Brunette' (zones 4 to 8) and *A. simplex* 'Hillside Black Beauty' (zones 4 to 8) provide rich mocha-purple foliage. As a whole, this brood goes by lots of common names, including snakeroot, cohosh, and fairy candles.

1. *Actaea* cultivar.

2. *Astilbe* 'Rhythm and Blues'.

Astilbe

Astilbe species and cultivars, zones 4 to 9
Summer (flowers)

Partial sun to shade; moist, fertile to average soil

Real flower color in shade is not just a pipe dream. Astilbes, also known as false spireas, display wonderful spires of color in early to midsummer—when all of the colorful, shade-loving spring blooms are long gone. The number of selections is astonishing as they provide flowers primarily in shades of white, lilac, pink, magenta, salmon, and red on plants that reach anywhere from 12 to 48 inches tall. Astilbes are great low-maintenance perennials with good disease and pest resistance. Plants typically have dark green, sometimes glossy, deeply cut foliage that forms a nice 1- to 2-foot-wide clump and supplies interesting texture for the entire growing season. The foliage has a soft appearance that means astilbes can be used like ferns as fillers and ground covers.

When in bloom, astilbe flowers create a striking mass of color on 6- to 24-inch-long stalks. Choosing a mix of early- and late-flowering varieties will result in an extended show. The blooms also make excellent cut flowers. Vigorous ground cover astilbes can be easily divided and moved around, which is great if you really want to cover an area. Most varieties do not like to dry out and will display crispy leaves if they do. *Astilbe chinensis* cultivars (zones 4 to 8), such as the gorgeous, 2-foot-tall 'Vision in Red', are usually the most drought tolerant. There are a great many hybrid cultivars. *Astilbe* ×*arendsii*

Brunnera macrophylla 'Jack Frost'.

'Ellie' (zones 4 to 8) has impressive white flowers, while A. 'Rhythm and Blues' (zones 4 to 8) features bright pink blooms. Both also average about 2 feet tall. Astilbes can do more than dress up the shade. They can also grow in full sun if planted in a spot with enough moisture, such as a low-lying or boggy area.

Brunnera

Brunnera macrophylla and cultivars, zones 3 to 7
Spring (flowers), spring to fall (foliage)

Partial shade; moist, well-drained, moderately fertile soil

In some areas, the solid green straight species runs quickly across the surface of moist, shady areas, displaying tiny blue flowers on stiff stems as they go in spring. From a distance they look very much like forget-me-nots (*Myosotis* species and cultivars, zones 3 to 9), but without the thick mass of strappy leaves. Brunneras sport fuzzy, heart-shaped leaves that eventually grow to form a clump 18 inches tall and wide. The rough texture of the foliage keeps it from being the snack du jour of young deer and rabbits. Thanks to the introduction of the cultivar 'Jack Frost', brunneras have spent some time in the spotlight. Its dazzling, silvery, green-veined leaves brighten up even the drabbest of settings.

Variegation is the big draw of these plants, and many cultivars offer a variation on this theme. Silver polka dots, white splashes, and soft yellow margins abound. Brunneras mix well with hostas (*Hosta* species and cultivars, zones 3 to 9) and ornamental grasses or sedges (*Carex* species and cultivars, zones 3 to 10) to weave a textural carpet under large trees. Plants do need consistent moisture, otherwise the leaves will burn around the edges, especially when exposed to too much sun or drought. Although they multiply modestly, variegated clumps can be readily divided and transplanted if you want more plants. For a change of pace, 'Betty Bowring' displays lovely white flowers above fresh, green foliage.

Hellebore
Helleborus species and cultivars, zones 4 to 9
Winter to spring (flowers), winter to fall (foliage)

Partial to full shade; moist, well-drained, fertile soil

It is not a stretch to say that hellebores are miracle plants. You would be hard-pressed to find other deer-, bunny-, groundhog-, and slug-resistant, disease-free, evergreen, winter-blooming, showy-leaved, sturdy perennials that prefer the dark corners of the garden. The most you may ever need to do to a hellebore, also know as Lenten rose or Christmas rose, is cut off any winter-damaged foliage in spring. The flower bracts stay attractive into late spring and early summer, long after the petals have disappeared. In their peak, the bracts appear in shades of green, white, pink, purple, and wine. The 1- to 3-inch-wide cups can set seed and self-sow in some cases. Hellebores typically form a mound 1 to 2 feet tall and wide. The leathery leaves are dark green to blue-green, deeply divided, and sometimes show a bit of silver variegation and veining.

Hellebores are native to Europe and Asia and are cherished collector plants. Many hybrids are available. The dif-

Helleborus
×*nigercors* 'HGC
Green Corsican'.

ferences may not be as apparent to the untrained eye, but the range of dizzying attributes includes doubled flowers, speckled petals, modified petal shapes, nodding and upward-facing flowers, and varying stem length and plant size. It is difficult to choose a favorite since they are basically all winners. *Helleborus* Ivory Prince (syn. *H.* 'Walhelivor', zones 4 to 8) is widely available due to its ease

Wet Feet

While a soggy site may be less than ideal, it is not the end of the world. Approach damp locations by finding plants that match the conditions, rather than trying to change the site. Lots of interesting choices are out there for wet soil in sun and shade. Stop swimming upstream, and embrace the wide world of plants that do not mind wet feet.

Planting Plan

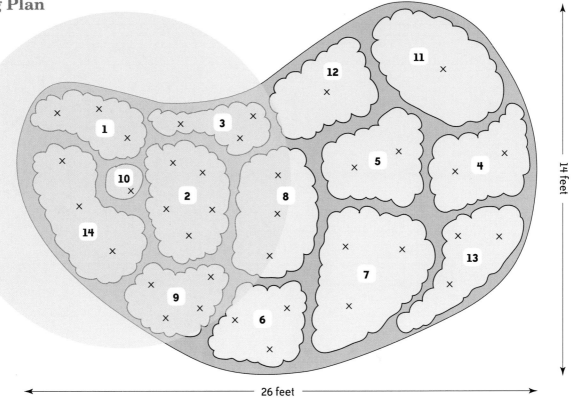

14 feet

26 feet

Plant List

1. *Astilbe* 'Deutschland' (zones 4 to 8).. 3 plants
2. *Athyrium filix-femina* (lady fern, zones 4 to 8)........................... 5 plants
3. *Chelone lyonii* 'Hot Lips' (turtlehead, zones 3 to 8)..................... 3 plants
4. *Helianthus angustifolius* 'Gold Lace' (sunflower, zones 5 to 9) ..... 2 plants
5. *Hibiscus coccineus* (swamp hibiscus, zones 7 to 9) .... 2 plants
6. *Iris ensata* 'Variegata' (Japanese iris, zones 4 to 9)...................... 3 plants
7. *Itea virginica* Little Henry
   (syn. *I. virginica* 'Sprich', Virginia sweetspire, zones 5 to 9) .... 3 plants
8. *Ligularia* 'Britt Marie Crawford' (zones 5 to 8)......................... 3 plants
9. *Lobelia cardinalis* (cardinal flower, zones 2 to 9) .... 4 plants
10. *Magnolia virginiana* Moonglow
    (syn. *M. virginiana* 'Jim Wilson', sweetbay magnolia, zones 5 to 9) .... 1 plant
11. *Metasequoia glyptostroboides* 'Jack Frost'
    (dawn redwood, zones 5 to 9) .... 1 plant
12. *Miscanthus sinensis* 'Gracillimus' (maiden grass, zones 5 to 9)....... 1 plant
13. *Physostegia virginiana* 'Rosea' (obedient plant, zones 3 to 9) .... 3 plants
14. *Rodgersia pinnata* 'Chocolate Wings' (zones 4 to 7)................. 3 plants

of propagation. Thankfully so, because it is a very attractive hellebore with silvery leaves and creamy, upright flowers. *Helleborus argutifolius* 'Janet Starnes' (zones 6 to 9) has appealing marbled foliage. *Helleborus ×nigercors* 'HGC Green Corsican' (zones 5 to 9) produces sophisticated, greenish white flowers, while *H.* Brandywine (zones 4 to 9) explodes with a cheery mix of flower colors and flower types.

Coral bell

Heuchera species and cultivars, zones 4 to 9
Spring to fall (foliage), summer (flowers)

Full sun to partial shade; moist, well-drained, fertile soil

Once upon a time there were only a few coral bell cultivars to choose from. Now there are so many it is hard to tell some of them apart. The best ones ensure low maintenance, provide blooms on sturdy stems for a long duration, offer interesting foliage, exhibit no disease or pest susceptibility, and are readily available in garden centers. All species form a well-behaved, mounding clump and work well as an edger or as a single specimen. Plants are also happy tucked into containers. The new, soft, fuzzy leaves pop out from the crown as soon as the soil warms in spring. As the rounded foliage matures it takes on a ruffled or jagged edge as plants eventually reach 12 to 36 inches tall and up to 36 inches wide by early summer, depending on the cultivar. Throughout summer, tiny red, pink, or white flower clusters form at the end of wiry stems. The blooms can be quite showy in the garden as well as in a cut flower arrangement.

The only maintenance coral bells require is a cutting back of the spent foliage and stems for the winter. Some gardeners in more temperate regions get to enjoy these plants as evergreens, however, with *Heuchera villosa* cultivars (zones 4 to 8) being an especially good choice for those folks. Choosing a favorite coral bell is no easy task. *Heuchera* 'Brownies' (zones 4 to 9) has beautifully warm brown tones that offer nice contrast to finely textured plants, while *H.* 'Green Spice' (zones 4 to 9) has silvery leaves with dark veins that contrast well with bolder plants like hellebores (*Helleborus* species and cultivars, zones 4 to 9). There are plenty to choose from on the wild side as well. Just to name a couple, *H.* 'Lime Rickey' (zones 4 to 8) has bright chartreuse foliage, and *H.* 'Georgia Peach' (zones 4 to 9) displays peachy leaves with a silvery overlay.

Hosta

Hosta species and cultivars, zones 3 to 9
Spring to fall (foliage), summer (flowers)

Full sun to full shade; moist, well-drained, fertile to average soil

If you cannot find a hosta that you like, you are just not a hosta person—literally thousands of these Asian superstars are on the market. Although hostas are often jokingly called "deer food," gardeners go to great lengths to use them any way they can to add a splash of foliage interest. The bold leaves are a designer's dream and can be used to enliven a mundane shade border, outline a dark path, create a massive ground cover, or add visual weight to a shady container. The novel leaves are quite varied, with miniature to gigantic sizes, matte or shiny surfaces, and smooth or puckered textures, with colors ranging from solid green to blue to yellow, often with variegation. Plant sizes vary drastically from 4-inch-tall-and-wide dwarfs to 3-foot-tall-and-wide (sometimes larger) behemoths. *Hosta* 'Sum and Substance' (zones 3 to 8) is a classic large, yellow-green variety; *H.* 'Halcyon' (zones 3 to 8) is a small, blue-green selection; and *H.* 'June' (zones 3 to 8) is a great medium-sized plant with gray-blue leaves that have a splash of yellow-green down the middle.

In summer, many hosta cultivars send up attractive stalks of waxy flowers that may or may not be fragrant. Some gardeners cut off the flowers, preferring a clean foliage-only look and missing out on all the beauty these plants have to offer. Hummingbirds are attracted to the blooms and make a nice garden accessory as they buzz in and out of the shade on a sunny day. Unfortunately, deer are not the only unwanted wildlife to enjoy the soft leaves and roots. Black weevils, cutworms, slugs, voles, rabbits, groundhogs, and squirrels can leave hostas chewed, shredded, upended, or just plain missing in one night. Sometimes the damage can be fixed by trimming the leaves. There are many pest control strategies out there, from spray repellents to physical barriers. It is good to mix up your tactics to confuse the beasts. In time, hostas will multiply to outgrow their space. Spring, before plants leaf out, is a good time to divide the dense rhizomes and share them with others. If you wait too long to divide old plants, you might need an ax.

Polygonatum odoratum 'Variegatum' (right) blends with an *Athyrium* cultivar (left of center) and *Hosta* cultivars (bottom and top left). Taken at The New York Botanical Garden.

Fragrant Solomon's seal
Polygonatum odoratum and cultivars, zones 3 to 8
Spring (flowers), spring to fall (foliage)

Partial to full shade; moist, well-drained, fertile to average soil

Elegant, arching stems come up from the rhizomes of this nearly perfect perennial. Fragrant Solomon's seal is a reliable choice for accenting shady spaces. Its smooth, elongated, 6-inch-long leaves march up the lengths with uniform regularity. The most widely found selection, 'Variegatum', features creamy white leaf margins and red-tinged stems. In midspring this species sends out small, 1-inch-long, white bells that dangle near the bottom of each leaf. They can emit noticeable, soft evening fragrance when planted in large enough groups. Fragrant Solomon's seal does not spread too quickly and can be easily divided before the leaves come up in spring. Plants look good from spring into fall, and you can never have too many. In fall the stems turn an attractive buttery yellow. Collectors might be interested in the double-flowering 'Flore Pleno', or 'Fireworks', a rare plant with yellow markings and white leaf margins. Fragrant Solomon's seal is not bothered by deer, but slugs can sometimes be a problem.

Lungwort
Pulmonaria species and cultivars, zones 2 to 8
Spring (flowers), spring to fall (foliage)

Partial to full shade; moist, well-drained, fertile to average soil

Silver foliage usually conjures up images of the desert, cactus gardens, or the seaside, but the silver-spotted leaves of lungworts are for the shade. Their bristly, medium green, oblong leaves vary in width and degree of silver blotchiness, from thin green straps to 6-inch-wide silver ovals. The habit is low growing and expands to a 12-inch-tall and 18- to 24-inch-wide mound. Lungworts produce tight clusters of pink to blue flowers that can begin in spring, just as the leaves appear. The flower buds are often a different color from the flowers, providing a multicolor effect. The splashy or polka-dotted foliage makes a good ground cover under trees.

It is easy to divide plants every few years to increase your area of coverage. They are susceptible to powdery mildew and slugs, and can look ratty by midsum-

1. *Pulmonaria* 'Roy Davidson' (bottom) and a *Deschampsia cespitosa* cultivar (center). Taken at the Brine Garden.

2. *Rodgersia pinnata* 'Superba'.

mer, but cutting the poor foliage away will bring fresh growth. The mildew does not kill the leaves, only disfigures them. Good winter drainage is a must if you want your plants to return the following year. Lungworts make exciting accents in a shade container and enjoy the perfect soil conditions there. Many selections are not happy in the heat and humidity of southern climates. Gardeners in those locales should choose more heat-tolerant varieties like *Pulmonaria* 'Roy Davidson' (zones 3 to 8). Other notable selections include *P. longifolia* 'Bertram Anderson' (zones 3 to 8) with long, narrow, silvery-spotted leaves and purple-blue blooms, and *P.* 'Silver Shimmers' (zones 4 to 8) with handsome, almost fully silver leaves and big blue flowers.

Rodgersia

Rodgersia species and cultivars, zones 3 to 8
Spring to fall (foliage), summer (flowers)

Partial shade; moist, fertile soil

Looking for something big and bold that the deer will not eat? Choose a rodgersia. These beauties hail from Asia and have palmate leaves that can easily span to 2 feet wide. Each leaf has five to nine crinkly, leatherlike, roughly 8-inch-long leaflets. Overall plant size can be 4 to 6 feet tall with an equal spread. They are magnificent plants for structure and large, contrasting texture. Depending on the species, ivory to rose red, fluffy panicle flowers top the stems in midsummer. They resemble the blooms of astilbes

(*Astilbe* species and cultivars, zones 4 to 9). You will not find rodgersias at every corner garden center, but they are gaining popularity. They tend to prefer wet, shady niches and are not at all happy in drier sites. Be sure to give plants plenty of elbow room. Probably one of the most interesting selections thus far is *Rodgersia pinnata* 'Chocolate Wings' (zones 4 to 7), which starts out the season with dark bronze leaves. Conversely, *R. podophylla* (zones 5 to 8) has leaves that turn bronze at the end of the season into fall.

Foamflower

Tiarella species and cultivars, zones 3 to 9
Spring to fall (foliage), spring to summer (flowers)

Partial to full shade; moist, fertile to average soil

In late spring and early summer, foamflower produces a frothy sea of white to pink with its bottlebrush blooms, each up to 8 inches long. The delicate-looking flowers maintain an upright form as they mingle with late-spring bulbs and other seasonal ephemerals. Tiarellas grow to about 12 inches tall and wide and make nice little ground covers or bed edgers. The show is not over after the flowers fade. Hairy, 4-inch-wide leaves have been hybridized to display a variety of color and shape variations that are a bit reminiscent of coral bells (*Heuchera* species and cultivars, zones 4 to 9). Many tiarella hybrids display deeply lobed leaves with dark maroon markings. The North American native *Tiarella cordifolia* (zones 3 to 8) has no doubt played a parenting role in the creation of many of the hybrids.

Its vigorous habit naturalizes beautifully across woodland floors. After a while the hybrids all start looking alike, but some continue to stand out. *Tiarella* 'Candy Stripper' (zones 4 to 9) and *T.* 'Black Snowflake' (zones 4 to 9) have finely cut leaves with dark markings down the finger-shaped lobes, while *T. cordifolia* 'Running Tapestry' (zones 4 to 8) has heart-shaped leaves with speckled red venation.

When grown in protected locations or in warmers zones, foamflowers can be evergreen. They are fairly trouble free and go unnoticed by deer and rabbits. Their markings can be less noticeable in nitrogen-rich soil, however. Some plants will run, while others are more clumping; choose a habit that best suits your needs.

Perennial TLC

Plant perennials at the same depth they were in their containers. Most perennials like a bit of organic matter. Turning some compost into the bed at planting time is not a bad idea. As with trees and shrubs, perennials appreciate supplemental water as they are becoming established in the first year. This is especially important during dry spells. A layer of mulch or composted leaf litter helps to retain soil moisture and suppress weeds. Just be sure to keep mulch a few inches away from perennial crowns to keep them from being at risk of rot. Plants that enjoy fertile soil can also be given an annual dose of organic fertilizer in the spring. Once established, perennials are fairly low maintenance.

1. To tidy things up, spent leaves and stems can be cut back in fall or early spring. Courtesy of Brent Benner.

GET OUT THE PRUNERS. Many perennials will reward you with more blooms if they are deadheaded. However, to avoid having to stay on top of this chore, it is always nice to just choose reblooming varieties like some geraniums. Many plants also benefit from a midseason trimming of tired leaves to encourage fresh new growth. In fall, herbaceous perennials can be cut back to the ground after a killing hard frost. This helps to get a jump start on spring cleanup and removes the dead leaves where slugs and other critters and diseases like to hide out over the winter. It is okay to leave some plants up until late spring, however. Grasses and plants with lingering seedheads, such as coneflowers, have ornamental value in the winter landscape.

KEEP BEASTS AT BAY. It is no secret that herbaceous plants can be particularly tasty to four-legged animals like deer and rabbits. If you have it in your budget, putting up fencing is a great way to keep these feeding machines at bay. Alternatively, various spray repellents can be used every few weeks to keep creatures away. Another good line of defense is to choose plants that animals do not like. This can be tricky since the menu is widely varied—what deer will avoid in one region is highly browsed in another. As a rule of thumb, however, deer do tend to avoid plants with strongly scented foliage, like artemisias, and those with fuzzy leaves, like lamb's ears.

2. Rabbit and deer damage can be prevented with the use of fencing and spray repellents.

PART THREE

THE SUPPORTING CAST

Summer-flowering bulbs like *Eucomis bicolor* 'Alba' add a little seasonal zip to plantings, especially when paired with the contrasting, deep purple foliage of *Oxalis triangularis* subsp. *papilionacea*. Courtesy of *Fine Gardening*, taken at Chanticleer Garden.

5

Bulbs

There is something magical about bulbs, even when they are just sitting in a mesh sack in a bin at the store. It is hard to believe that such a riot of seasonal color can be produced by these seemingly lifeless, onionlike spheres. No mixed bed or border is complete without these seductive ephemerals.

Allium species and cultivars trickled through a mixed border provide unique appeal even after the blooms fade and dry. Taken at Chanticleer Garden.

Their annual show may be fleeting, but if you play your cards right, you will have no shortage of timely bulb flower color—just choose a mix of varieties that will take turns strutting their stuff throughout the year.

ALLIUM RULES THE ROOST

Allium species and cultivars, zones 2 to 11
Spring to fall (flowers), summer to fall (seedheads)

Full sun, with some species tolerant of shade; moderately moist, well-drained, fertile soil

As far as bulbs go, alliums or ornamental onions are among the best for extended seasonal interest and deer resistance. This vast genus contains a wide variety of species and cultivars, including some North American natives like tapertip onion (*Allium acuminatum*, zones 3 to 9) and nodding onion (*A. cernuum*, zones 3 to 9). Careful selection will ensure that you have blooms in spring, summer, and fall. Their characteristic floral starbursts can range from the size of a small cherry tomato to a large cantaloupe in shades of white, pink, purple, and yellow. The flowers sit on stems that also vary in height, anywhere from 4 to 48 inches tall, which makes these bulbs suitable for the front, middle, and back of the border. After the flowers fade, the seedheads provide killer structural interest long after the leaves have shriveled up and the bulbs have hit the hay for the rest of the year.

Once spring is well underway, alliums start to explode with color. The Persian onion *Allium hollandicum* 'Purple Sensation' (syn. *A. aflatunense* 'Purple Sensa-

Allium hollandicum 'Purple Sensation' (syn. *A. aflatunense* 'Purple Sensation').

tion', zones 4 to 8) is a classic late-spring selection that can reach up to 3 feet tall with brilliant royal purple blooms about the size of a tennis ball. Star of Persia (*A. cristophii*, zones 4 to 8) is another crowd pleaser, opening on 12- to 24-inch-tall stems in early summer. Its flowers are not as dense or intensely colored, but they certainly create quite a buzz, forming airy, 5- to 8-inch-round spheres in shades of silvery purple. The dried seedheads are almost as intriguing as the fresh blooms and sometimes tumble around the garden creating eye-catching combos.

Golden onion (*Allium moly*, zones 3 to 9) enters the stage in midsummer with lemon yellow flowers that are about the size of a ping-pong ball and stand on 12-inch-tall stems. Besides its unusual color, this species is also handy for its tolerance of shade.

To end the gardening season with a bang, give the Japanese onion *Allium thunbergii* 'Ozawa' (zones 4 to 9) a shot. This autumn beauty grows up to 12 inches tall and produces spectacular 1- to 2-inch-round, violet-red blooms. It is hard not to do a double take when you see it in action.

Of course, if none of these selections strike your fancy, there are many, many more alliums to be sought out and enjoyed. These are just scratching the surface.

THE BIG THREE

Grown in cultivation for centuries, lilies, daffodils, and tulips have become "the big three" of gardening bulbs. They are tried-and-true, with wonderful diversity. Stalwart varieties have stood the test of time, while breeders keep things exciting with new introductions each year. The options truly seem endless. When putting together mixed plantings, do not forget to include at least one or two groupings of these longtime favorites.

Lily

Lilium species and cultivars, zones 2 to 9
Summer (flowers)

Full sun, with some species and hybrids tolerant of partial shade; moist, extremely well drained, fertile soil

Lilies in the garden are like that colorful great aunt during the holidays—utterly unforgettable. Frequently decked in the brightest and wildest of colors, these summer-blooming flowers pack a visual punch and often make their presence known with an intense perfume. The color, size, and petal curvature of the flowers vary depending on the selection. There is a lily out there to suit every taste, from gaudy orange to delicate pink. Several species, such as Canada lily (*Lilium canadense*, zones 3 to 8) and wood lily (*L. philadelphicum*, zones 3 to 8), are native to North America. Lilies are divided into nine categories, with Asiatic and Oriental being among the most popular among gardeners (and, unfortunately, deer). Stems can reach from 1 to 8 feet tall and sometimes need staking to support their exuberant blooms. The show is well worth the effort. The gigantic, fragrant, white flowers of *L.* 'Casa Blanca' (zones 5 to 8) are indeed a sight to be seen, and smelled, in summer. At 4 feet tall, they work well at the back of the border. Fragrant *L.* 'Star Gazer' (zones 3 to 8) also creates quite a visual frenzy in summer with speckled, dark rosy pink blooms edged in white on 3- to 5-foot-tall stems. The great thing about lilies having slender stems is that the plants can easily be tucked into borders where they will fade into the background when the show is over.

Daffodil

Narcissus species and cultivars, zones 3 to 9
Spring (flowers)

Full sun; moist, well-drained, moderately fertile soil

These quintessential bulbs are the harbingers of the gardening season, dancing across the somewhat barren spring landscape with sunny yellow smiles. *Narcissus* is a huge genus split into twelve groups, each with many different flower shapes, sizes, colors, and bloom timing. This easygoing brood collectively features trumpet, large-cupped, small-cupped, double, nodding, and petite blooms, which can be up to 5 inches across. The flowers come in lovely shades of white, yellow, and orange and open from mid- to late spring. The bulbs can naturalize into clumps that typically stand anywhere from 3 to 24 inches tall, depending on the variety, and are not on the Bambi menu. Pheasant's eye (*N. poeticus* var. *recurvus*, zones 3 to 7) is a classic, fragrant species with simple, pure white petals that circle a small yellow cup with a red rim. *Narcissus* 'Serola' (zones 4 to 8) produces bright blossoms with golden yellow petals and a red-orange center. There are literally thousands of *Narcissus* to choose from. The most difficult thing about this genus is deciding which ones to grow.

1. *Lilium* 'Casa Blanca'.

2. *Narcissus* 'Serola'.

Gardeners in warm climates have lots of fun summer-heat-loving bulbs to choose from. Although some of these plants technically grow from corms or fleshy roots, not bulbs, they are included in the bulb category. Regardless of what root structure they grow from, they put on a pretty incredible display. If you live in a cold climate, do not feel left out. You can grow these plants as annuals or go the extra mile and bring them inside for the winter. Tender bulbs can be grown in a pot, or lifted out of the ground, and stored in a cool (typically 40°F to 50°F), dry basement, root cellar, sunroom, or garage. Consider a mix of these red-hot favorites for your garden's hot, sunny locations.

Crinum **species and cultivars** (Cape coast lily, zones 7 to 11)
Crocosmia **species and cultivars** (zones 6 to 10)
Eucomis **species and cultivars** (pineapple lily, zones 7 to 11)
Gladiolus **species and cultivars** (zones 6 to 10)
Hedychium **species and cultivars** (ginger lily, zones 7 to 11)
Hymenocallis **species and cultivars** (spider lily, zones 6 to 11)
Lycoris **species** (resurrection lily, spider lily, zones 6 to 11)
Nerine **species and cultivars** (zones 8 to 10)
Tritonia **species and cultivars** (zones 7 to 10)
Zephyranthes **species and cultivars** (zephyr lily, zones 7 to 11)

1. *Crocosmia* ×*crocosmiiflora* 'Solfatare'. Courtesy of Terra Nova Nurseries.

2. *Hedychium coccineum* 'Tara'.

Getting Bulbs Off to a Good Start

The trick to planting bulbs is setting them at the right depth. If you get it wrong, you may end up with a whole lot of nothing. Each bulb is different, so pay attention to depth recommendations on plant labels. Recommended depths can range anywhere from two to four times the size of the bulb. The best time to plant spring-flowering bulbs is in autumn, six weeks before the ground freezes and turns hard as a rock. Summer bulbs can be planted outdoors in spring once temperatures remain consistently around 55°F. They can also be started earlier in spring in containers indoors to get them jumpstarted and ready roll.

Bulb leaves soak up energy for flowers. Avoid cutting them back prematurely.

PICK THE RIGHT TOOL. Many handy bulb-planting tools are available. Choosing the right one comes down to personal preference. Digging by hand with a dibble (for small bulbs), trowel, or bulb planter can be very rewarding. For big jobs, using an electric- or gas-powered auger or shovel (to dig trenches) might be more appropriate. Either way, avoid planting bulbs in rows. It looks much more natural and attractive to place them in randomly spaced groups.

SUPPLY AN ANNUAL FEEDING. There are several schools of thought when it comes to feeding bulbs. To help bulbs settle in, it is not a bad idea to mix a dose of a phosphorus-rich amendment into the hole. This will help to establish strong root growth. After the first year, give your bulbs an annual fall feeding with a topdressing of compost or well-balanced fertilizer. Heavy feeders, such as tulips, sometimes benefit from two applications of fertilizer, one in spring and another in autumn.

RESPOND TO THEIR NEEDS. Even though it is extremely difficult, resist the temptation to cut back the unattractive fading foliage until it is completely yellow. Bulbs rely on the energy collected by the leaves after flowering to produce the next year's floral display. If you notice that flowering is decreasing over time, it is probably time to divide your bulbs. Lifting, splitting, and replanting large clumps every four to five years will keep the bulbs vigorous and productive.

Tulipa 'Garant'. Courtesy of *Fine Gardening*, taken at the Sternberg Garden.

Tulip

Tulipa species and cultivars, zones 3 to 8
Spring (flowers)

Full sun; moderately moist, sharply draining, fertile soil

Tulips are not just for people with wooden shoes and windmills. They come in just about every color under the sun and have been viewed as trophy flowers since the days of the early explorers. Like daffodils, tulips offer many flower shapes and sizes, which shine on 6- to 30-inch-tall stems in mid- to late spring. They are broken down into fifteen groups. Traditional cup-shaped blooms as well as fringed, double, and star-shaped varieties are popular choices. The flowers can average 3 to 5 inches across. Tulips can be the most finicky of the classic bulbs, and usually only have one or two good years in them. They are often grown as annuals, especially in areas where this genus falls victim to inadequate cool temperatures, poor drainage, disease, or hungry wildlife. However, their powerful spring punch is well worth the extra effort. For extended interest, tulips with variegated or mottled leaves are the best choice—you get a fantastic spring display when they are in and out of bloom. *Tulipa* 'Garant' has slender leaves outlined in yellow with matching crisp yellow blossoms. *Tulipa* 'Calypso' sports red-orange flowers above green leaves with wine-red pinstripes, while *T.* 'Carnaval de Nice' is a bit more refined, featuring fine, white leaf margins and white blooms splashed with burgundy.

UNSUNG HEROES

Because the classic bulbs often get top billing, many other garden-worthy bulbs fall off our radar. They may not have the same bold attributes as daffodils, tulips, or lilies, but these gems can hold their own, providing unique, tantalizing displays. When filling your mixed border dance card, include at least one of these bulbs in the lineup. You will be pleasantly surprised.

Camas

Camassia species and cultivars, zones 3 to 9
Spring to summer (flowers)

Full sun to partial shade; moist, well-drained, fertile soil; tolerant of wet conditions in spring

Camas bulbs send up beautiful blue, purple, and white flower spikes from late spring to early summer. Once a vital food source for Native Americans, Western explorers, and settlers, these North American natives are gaining popularity in cultivated gardens. The 8- to 20-inch-long flower stalks mingle well with other herbaceous plants in borders. They are not favored by deer and do not overstay their welcome. They are quick to go dormant after setting seed, so you do not have to look at yellowing leaves for weeks on end. Reaching 12 to 36 inches tall, camas bulbs can be planted in the front and middle of the border. The pale to deep blue hues of *Camassia cusickii* and cultivars (zones 3 to 8) are hard to resist in the spring garden. You can give plantings a pop of white with the gorgeous flower spikes of *C. leichtlinii* 'Semiplena' (zones 4 to 8), while *C. quamash* 'Blue Melody' (zones 4 to 8) offers a little change of pace with creamy-edged leaves accompanied by dark purple-blue blooms.

Camassia leichtlinii cultivar. Taken at Hollister House Garden.

A Golden Touch

Lucky for us, King Midas did not corner the market on the golden touch. Plant breeders continue to bring us loads of plants with gorgeous golden leaves. From trees and shrubs to annuals and perennials, it is easy to find a touch of gold for the garden. This rich color punches up any landscape and looks breathtaking when accentuated by blue and burgundy tones in nearby flowers and leaves. Gold brightens up any setting, in sun or shade. Just do not forget to throw in a little contrast—there is such a thing as too much gold.

Planting Plan

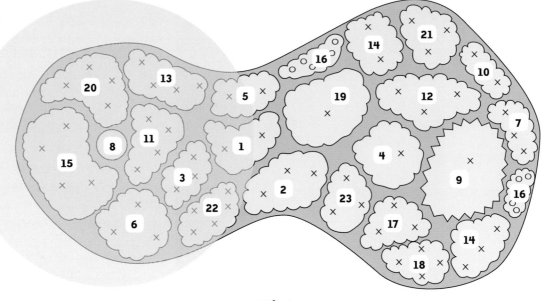

14 feet

30 feet

Plant List

1 *Agastache* 'Blue Fortune' (anise hyssop, zones 5 to 9) . 2 plants

2 *Alternanthera dentata* 'Rubiginosa' (zones 10 to 11) 3 plants

3 *Astrantia* 'Moulin Rouge' (masterwort, zones 4 to 7)... 3 plants

4 *Baptisia* 'Purple Smoke' (wild indigo, zones 4 to 9)..... 1 plant

5 *Campanula poscharskyana* 'Blue Waterfall' (bellflower, zones 3 to 7)..................................... 2 plants

6 *Carex* 'Red Rooster' (sedge, zones 6 to 9) .... 3 plants

7 *Ceratostigma plumbaginoides* (plumbago, zones 5 to 9) .... 3 plants

8 *Cercis canadensis* 'Hearts of Gold' (redbud, zones 5 to 9) .... 1 plant

9 *Cornus alternifolia* Gold Bullion (syn. *C. alternifolia* 'Bachone', pagoda dogwood, zones 3 to 7) .... 1 plant

10 *Cosmos atrosanguineus* (chocolate cosmos, zones 7 to 9) .... 2 plants

11 *Dryopteris erythrosora* 'Brilliance' (autumn fern, zones 5 to 9) .... 4 plants

12 *Foeniculum vulgare* 'Smokey' (bronze fennel, zones 6 to 9)..................................... 3 plants

13 *Hakonechloa macra* 'All Gold' (Japanese forest grass, zones 5 to 9) .... 4 plants

14 *Hemerocallis* 'Midnight Magic' (daylily, zones 3 to 10)... 5 plants

15 *Hypericum calycinum* 'Brigadoon' (St. John's wort, zones 5 to 7).................................. 4 plants

16 *Narcissus* 'Serola' (daffodil, zones 4 to 8) .... 10 plants

17 *Pennisetum purpureum* 'Princess' (purple fountain grass, zones 8 to 11)......................... 3 plants

18 *Sedum rupestre* 'Angelina' (zones 6 to 9) .... 4 plants

19 *Spiraea thunbergii* Mellow Yellow (syn. *S. thunbergii* 'Ogon', zones 4 to 8)........................ 1 plant

20 *Tiarella* 'Cygnet' (foamflower, zones 4 to 9)............... 4 plants

21 *Verbascum* 'Honey Dijon' (mullein, zones 5 to 9) ... 3 plants

22 *Veronica spicata* 'Glory' (syn. *V. spicata* 'Royal Candles', speedwell, zones 3 to 8).... 5 plants

23 *Yucca filamentosa* 'Color Guard' (hardy yucca, zones 5 to 10).. 3 plants

Crocus
Crocus species and cultivars, zones 3 to 9
Spring and fall (flowers)

Full sun to partial shade; moist, well-drained, poor to moderately fertile soil

Probably a bit better known than some of the other unsung heroes, *Crocus* delivers on diversity with an extensive membership of species and cultivars. Even better, this group offers spring- and autumn-flowering choices and is seldom chomped on by deer. Because plenty of other bulbs flower in the spring, it is not a bad idea to put all your "crocus eggs" in the fall basket. Crocuses usually reach 2 to 6 inches tall and bloom in shades of pink, purple, yellow, and white. The cup-shaped flowers can be up to 2 inches long. Plant them tightly in groups to create pockets of cheery color at the front of the border. *Crocus ochroleucus* (zones 5 to 9) delivers lovely, creamy white flowers in late autumn. For a little more color, choose blue *C. speciosus* 'Conqueror' (zones 4 to 8), which also flowers in fall. If you want to put a little spring crocus in your step, spruce up grassy areas or the lawn with spring bloomers like orange-flowering *C. chrysanthus* 'Zwanenburg Bronze' (zones 3 to 8).

Snowdrop
Galanthus species and cultivars, zones 3 to 8
Winter to spring (flowers)

Partial shade; moderately moist, well-drained, fertile soil

It is hard not to be impressed by snowdrops. These diminutive, deer-resistant gems bloom in late winter and early spring, when few other plants are doing much of anything. Their bell-shaped flowers average about an inch long and blanket the ground when plants are allowed to naturalize on the woodland floor or in grassy meadows. Plants only reach 3 to 10 inches tall in bloom. Because of their small size, snowdrops are best enjoyed at the edge of a bed where they can be observed in more formal plantings. There are several species and cultivars to choose from. Usually only collectors can recognize the subtle differences, but giant snowdrop (*Galanthus elwesii* and cultivars) is an exception that is easy to recognize for its larger flowers, up to 2 inches long. Some selections, such as *G. nivalis* 'Flore Pleno', also stand out for their double flowers. Green markings

1. *Galanthus elwesii.*

2. *Muscari aucheri* 'Blue Magic'.

on the tips of the petals give *G. nivalis* 'Viridapice' a unique look. Even so, the nodding white blooms of any of the plants in this genus are a welcome sight in the dawn of spring.

Grape hyacinth

Muscari species and cultivars, zones 2 to 9
Spring (flowers)

Full sun; moist but not wet, well-drained, moderately fertile soil

It is often love at first sight when we see these little bulbs in bloom. When grape hyacinth is planted in groups and left to naturalize, masses of petite purple and blue spikes wow audiences in midspring. A few atypical selections, such as *Mus-cari aucheri* 'White Magic' (zones 4 to 9), come in white. You may also be able to turn up a rare pink or yellow selection. Grape hyacinths typically grow around 4 to 8 inches tall with flower spikes up to 3 inches long, depending on the variety. They make good edging plants and go unnoticed by deer. If you choose a few early- and late-flowering selections, you can kick back and admire the show for weeks. The sky blue flowers, dressed with dark blue stripes, of *M. azureum* (zones 4 to 9) are among the first to appear in early spring. In midspring the plump, rich blue flowers of *M. aucheri* 'Blue Magic' (zones 4 to 9) open along with the lovely, pale blue blossoms of *M. armeniacum* 'Valerie Finnis' (zones 4 to 8), which will carry the display a little further.

Going Native

Choosing native plants is a great way to create a more low-maintenance, sustainable garden. These plants already know the ropes and have acclimated to your climate. They tend to need minimal supplemental water once established and tolerate local adverse conditions. A mixed native border with a succession of blooms will offer color from spring to fall. Placing a native border in a sunny spot off a deck or patio is a great way to have a comfortable vantage point from where you can observe birds, butterflies, and any other wildlife that benefits from your plant choices. The planting scheme shown here features a reliable mix of North American natives that are readily available.

Planting Plan

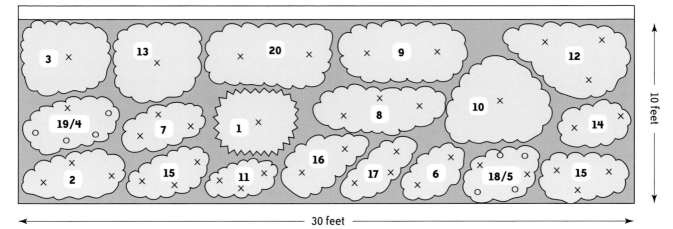

30 feet

10 feet

Plant List

1 *Abies concolor* 'Compacta' (compact white fir, zones 4 to 7) .... 1 plant

2 *Amsonia* 'Blue Ice' (bluestar, zones 4 to 9) .... 3 plants

3 *Baptisia* ×*varicolor* 'Twilite'
(Prairieblues series, wild indigo, zones 4 to 8) .... 1 plant

4 *Camassia leichtlinii* 'Semiplena' (camas, zones 4 to 8) .... 4 plants

5 *Camassia leichtlinii* subsp. *suksdorfii* 'Blue Danube'
(syn. *C. leichtlinii* subsp. *suksdorfii* 'Blauwe Donau', camas, zones 4 to 8).. 4 plants

6 *Coreopsis* 'Jethro Tull' (tickseed, zones 5 to 8) .... 2 plants

7 *Echinacea* Harvest Moon (Big Sky series, syn. *E.* 'Matthew Saul',
coneflower, zones 5 to 8) .... 3 plants

8 *Eupatorium dubium* 'Little Joe' (Joe-Pye weed, zones 4 to 8) .... 3 plants

9 *Helianthus* 'Lemon Queen' (sunflower, zones 4 to 9) .... 2 plants

10 *Itea virginica* 'Henry's Garnet' (sweetspire, zones 5 to 9) .... 1 plant

11 *Liatris spicata* 'Kobold' (blazing star, zones 3 to 9) .... 3 plants

12 *Panicum virgatum* 'Northwind' (switch grass, zones 4 to 9)........... 3 plants

13 *Physocarpus opulifolius* 'Diablo' (ninebark, zones 3 to 8)............. 1 plant

14 *Rudbeckia triloba* (three-lobed coneflower, zones 3 to 10) .... 2 plants

15 *Salvia farinacea* 'Victoria' (mealy-cup sage, zones 9 to 11) .... 6 plants

16 *Schizachyrium scoparium* 'The Blues'
(little blue stem, zones 3 to 9).. 2 plants

17 *Stokesia laevis* 'Peachie's Pick' (Stokes' aster, zones 5 to 9) .... 3 plants

18 *Symphyotrichum laevis* 'Bluebird'
(syn. *Aster laevis* 'Bluebird', smooth aster, zones 4 to 8)...................... 2 plants

19 *Symphyotrichum* 'Wood's Pink'
(syn. *Aster* 'Wood's Pink', aster, zones 5 to 8) .... 1 plant

20 *Veronicastrum virginicum* (Culver's root, zones 3 to 9)................. 2 plants

Bedfellows for Bulbs

Bulbs provide the greatest impact when planted in groups—as with other garden plants, they get lost in the crowd when planted one here and one there. The key to accenting the garden with bulbs, however, is to also pair them with herbaceous bedfellows that will fill the gaps bulbs leave once they go dormant. There is nothing worse than big gaping holes at the front of a bed where glorious daffodils or tulips stood earlier in the season. Fast-growing annuals fill this role beautifully, as do choice hardy perennial selections. Here are some excellent bedfellow candidates.

Annual cohorts

***Begonia* species and cultivars** (zones 9 to 11, partial shade)

***Gomphrena globosa* and cultivars** (globe amaranth, annual, full sun)

***Impatiens* species and cultivars** (zones 10 to 11, partial shade)

***Nicotiana* species and cultivars** (flowering tobacco, zones 10 to 11, full sun)

***Salvia* species and cultivars** (tropical sage, zones 7 to 11, full sun)

***Solenostemon scutellarioides* cultivars** (coleus, zones 10 to 11, full sun to partial shade)

Perennial partners

***Brunnera macrophylla* cultivars** (zones 3 to 7, shade)

***Geranium* species and cultivars** (zones 3 to 9, full sun to partial shade)

***Hemerocallis* species and cultivars** (daylily, zones 3 to 10, full sun)

***Heuchera* species and cultivars** (coral bell, zones 3 to 9, partial shade)

***Lamium* species and cultivars** (dead nettle, zones 4 to 8, shade)

***Nepeta* species and cultivars** (catmint, zones 3 to 9, full sun)

Gomphrena 'Strawberry Fields'. Taken at Central Park Conservatory Garden.

(right) *Nepeta sibirica*. Taken at Cornell Plantations.

6

Annuals and Tropicals

Although they only last one gardening season, annuals and tropicals are worth their weight in gold in the garden. They rarely take a breather from the time you set them out until the first hard autumn frost zaps them.

Pockets of tropicals like *Colocasia esculenta* 'Black Magic' (top), an *Ipomoea batatas* cultivar (left of center), a *Gomphrena* cultivar (center), a *Nicotiana* cultivar (right of center), *Solenostemon scutellarioides* 'Dark Star' (bottom left), and a *Pelargonium* cultivar (bottom right) energize summer plantings. Taken at Central Park Conservatory Garden.

Their fabulous foliage and abundant blooms seamlessly thread plantings together with rich colors and textures. Because most annuals and tropicals are fast growers and flowering machines, they need good, fertile soil (or regular feedings) and occasional pinching and deadheading—a small price to pay for such big rewards. Once you get the hang of it, choosing the right tender gems for your garden is easy. Begin by selecting flower and leaf colors that echo those already present in your woody plants and perennials. As you become more comfortable and adventurous, experiment with bold, contrasting color combinations. Likewise, pick plants that will provide a mix of distinct coarse, medium, and fine textures.

As with the term *perennial*, the word *annual* defines a plant's life cycle. True annuals sprout, grow, form flowers, produce seed, and die all in one year. Over time, plants that are not cold hardy to an area (and must be planted every year to be enjoyed) have been lumped into this category—even though they are truly perennial in their native habitat. As a result, exotic plants that just do not like the cold are sometimes called tropicals and tender perennials as well as annuals. If it dies in the winter in your area, go ahead and call it an annual.

BIG AND BOLD

Large tropicals are the ultimate botanical eye candy. Their exaggerated features get lots of head turns, making them the perfect seasonal specimen plants. Most of the big guns want full sun, regular moisture, and of course plenty of nutrients. If you are planting these beauties directly in the ground, start them out in good loam that has been fortified with compost and perhaps a slow-release fertilizer. If you are growing them in containers, start them off with a granular slow-release fertilizer and give them a light feeding of diluted water-soluble fertilizer every few weeks during the growing season. Most soilless container mixes contain very few nutrients. Growing these plants in containers is often the preferred way to go. In pots, they can be easily moved around, slipped into borders, and brought inside to overwinter.

Elephant's ear

Alocasia species and cultivars, zones 8 to 11
Spring to fall (foliage)
Colocasia species and cultivars, zones 8 to 11
Spring to fall (foliage)

Full sun to partial shade; moist to wet, fertile soil

The fantastically massive forms of elephant's ears are definitely hard to miss in the garden. Their elongate, heart-shaped leaves can grow to about the size of a pillow case, sometimes even larger, while their color can range from bright green to deep purple (almost black) with some exquisite leaf veining and variegation, as in the white-splotched *Alocasia* 'Hilo Beauty' (zones 9 to 11). Smaller options offer leaves about the size of your hand, such as *Colocasia affinis* var. *jeningsii* (zones 8 to 11), which has amazing dark bronzy leaves with bright green veins and highlights. Give gigantic elephant's ears plenty of elbow room. Depending on the variety, these tropical perennials can produce an 18-inch-tall-and-wide clump all the way up to a 6-foot-tall-and-wide

Colocasia affinis var. *jeningsii*.

stand that can grow even larger in southern climates. 'Black Magic' and 'Illustris' are two popular cultivars of *C. esculenta* (zones 8 to 11) that grow on the large end of the size spectrum. 'Illustris' also has bronzy leaves with green highlights, while 'Black Magic' has intense deep purple, almost black, leaves. Elephant's ears like these are great as centerpieces at the back of the border; smaller varieties work well front and center. You can intensify their drama by pairing them with finely textured plants. They typically go unnoticed by deer. If your area is prone to lots of hail, which will shred the leaves, elephant's ears are probably not for you. Otherwise, keep in mind that *Colocasia* varieties can take fairly wet conditions, while *Alocasia* selections require good drainage.

Angel's trumpet

Brugmansia species and cultivars, zones 8 to 11
Summer (flowers)

Full sun; moist, well-drained, fertile soil

Seeing angel's trumpet in bloom will make anyone do a double take. The remarkable, trumpet-shaped flowers can reach from 6 to 10 inches long (possibly larger) in pleasing shades of white, yellow, or pink. The blooms dangle from 3- to 10-foot-tall, fast-growing plants that typically spread to half as wide. Angel's trumpets are technically trees and shrubs; they grow significantly larger in their native habitat of South America. The leaves average anywhere from 6 to 12 inches long and are deer resistant. To mix things up, keep an eye out for variegated cultivars like *Brugmansia* 'Snowbank' with creamy white leaf margins. Depending

1. *Brugmansia* 'Jamaican Yellow'.

2. *Canna* 'Pretoria' (syn. *C.* 'Bengal Tiger' and *C.* 'Striata'). Taken at The New York Botanical Garden.

on the variety, the flowers are fragrant in the early evening. The creamy yellow blooms of *B.* 'Jamaican Yellow' (zones 9 to 11) and bubblegum pink *B.* 'Pink Beauty' (zones 9 to 11) both provide wonderful fragrance. Even without a scent, however, these plants are enchanting. You must invest a healthy amount water and fertilizer to get this payoff, but it is well worth it. Few things are greater than enjoying angel's trumpet from the vantage point of a favorite outdoor lounger with a special summer-evening beverage in hand. Just don't get any pieces of the plant in your glass—this beauty is poisonous.

Canna

Canna species and cultivars, zones 7 to 11
Spring to fall (foliage), summer to fall (flowers)

Full sun; moist, fertile soil

"Wallflower" is definitely something you would never call a canna. While this tender perennial certainly grows well up against a sunny wall, it is anything but shy or reserved. As a group, cannas scream out for attention with their brightly colored blooms and big, sometimes striped leaves. The flowers come in wild shades of yellow, orange, red, and pink, while the foliage can be green, blue-green, deep burgundy, or a combination of green with yellow or apricot-orange variegation. *Canna* 'Pretoria' (syn. *C.* 'Bengal Tiger' and *C.* 'Striata', zones 7 to 11) is a screamer with bright orange flow-

Ensete ventricosum 'Maurelii' (top left) combined with *Physocarpus opulifolius* 'Diablo' (left of center), *Stachys byzantina* 'Big Ears' (syn. *S. byzantina* 'Countess Helen von Stein', bottom left), and *Perovskia atriplicifolia* (bottom right). Taken at Chanticleer Garden.

ers that mingle with yellow-and-green-striped leaves. More reserved options include *C.* 'President' (zones 7 to 11) with blue-green foliage and rich red blooms, and *C.* 'Constitution' (zones 8 to 11) with glaucous purple leaves and soft pink flowers. Cannas typically grow 4 to 6 feet tall and 2 feet wide with leaves that can reach to 2 feet long. They are true fifty-mile-per-hour plants, often seen growing in highway medians in the southern United States. They add flair to any border or container and happily mingle with other sun-loving plants. Deer seldom like cannas, but plants can occasionally suffer from a fungal or viral disease. Feed cannas regularly through the growing season and remove spent blooms to keep them healthy and encourage encore floral displays.

Banana

Ensete ventricosum and cultivars, zones 9 to 11
Spring to fall (foliage)
Musa species and cultivars, zones 7 to 11
Spring to fall (foliage)

Full sun to partial shade; moderately moist, well-drained, fertile soil

Nothing says tropical more than bananas. These exotic plants send up huge, paddle-like leaves that are sometimes cast in coppery red, depending on the variety. While bananas can average 20 feet tall and 10 feet wide in the tropics, they generally grow to about half that size in less temperate climates. Where they are native, in places like Africa and Asia, bananas are perennials with leaves that can grow to the size of small surfboards or larger. They make superb focal points in beds around patios or in large, hefty containers. They have a broad canopy and narrow base that allows plenty of room for other showy plants to grow at their feet. Plants do not mind a little afternoon shade, but keep them protected from strong winds or their leaves will become rather tattered.

Gardeners have had fun experimenting with the hardiness of bananas. *Musa basjoo* (zones 7 to 11) is among the hardiest species, with reports of plants dying back to the ground like traditional perennials when planted in microclimates and given heavy winter mulch in zones 4 to 6. *Ensete ventricosum* and its cultivars (zones 9 to 11) are among the more ornamental options. 'Maurelii' has wonderful leaves cast in coppery red. *Musa acuminata* (zones 10 to 11) is one of the common producers of the fruit that we find in the grocery store. 'Dwarf Cavendish' is a dwarf cultivar that grows 5 to 10 feet tall. Unfortunately, in the United States, gardeners in Florida are among the few who get to successfully enjoy banana flowers and fruit in their own backyards. That is okay, though—the plants still look pretty nifty in beds and borders and do not seem to be on the deer menu.

Tropical hibiscus

Hibiscus species and cultivars, zones 9 to 11
Summer to fall (flowers)

Full sun; moist, well-drained, fertile soil

With more than 200 species in the genus *Hibiscus*, you are bound to find one you like. While many hardy species are available, some of the more exotic ones will really knock your socks off. *Hibiscus rosa-sinensis* (zones 9 to 11) is a popular tropi-

Hibiscus rosa-sinensis 'The Path'.

cal shrub species that offers endless cultivars with big flowers, like the 4-inch-wide blooms of 'The Path' (zones 10 to 11), a magnificent selection with orange-yellow petals that meet at a hot pink center. The blooms of hibiscus almost look too good to be true. They resemble party favors made from brightly colored crepe paper in shades of red, orange, pink, yellow, and white. Most tropical hibiscus range from 3 to 10 feet tall and half as wide.

The jumbo (up to 6 inches across), sometimes garish flowers of hibiscus are not for everyone. Thankfully, other great options sit on the opposite end of the wild, colorful spectrum. *Hibiscus acetosella* and cultivars (zones 9 to 11) feature wonderful maplelike leaves and smaller, more subtle flowers in shades of pink. 'Panama Red', a remarkable introduction with wine-red leaves, is a great addition to any combination.

As with other tropicals, hibiscus are dazzling in beds or containers. They love the heat but can occasionally run into

Some Like It Hot

Jazz up the garden with vibrant hues. Brilliant reds, yellows, and oranges will brighten up even the cloudiest of days. A vivid color palette is also a great way to enliven an outdoor entertainment space. Look for eye-popping colors in both flowers and foliage, with dark-colored companions to provide a nice contrast. Including a mix of woody plants, perennials, bulbs, annuals, and tropicals will extend the show throughout summer. Consider adding a pergola with a vigorous vine to your design to give you and your guests a little relief from the hot summer sun while you enjoy the riot of color.

Planting Plan

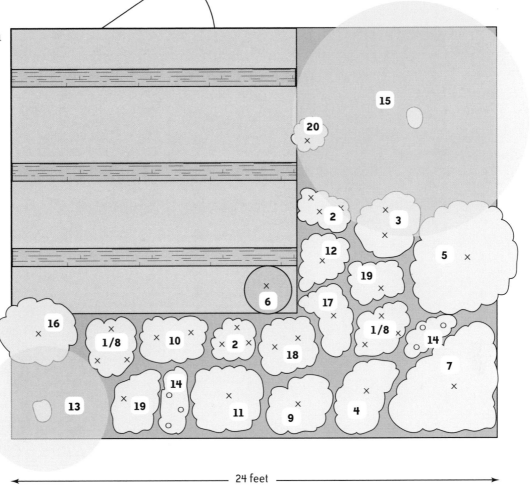

20 feet

24 feet

Plant List

1. *Abutilon* 'Voodoo' (flowering maple, zones 8 to 11) ..... 1 plant
2. *Angelonia* Angelface Blue (syn. *A*. 'Anzwei', zones 9 to 11) .... 6 plants
3. *Canna* 'King Midas' (syn. *C*. 'Richard Wallace', zones 7 to 11) .... 2 plants
4. *Colocasia esculenta* 'Elena' (elephant's ear, zones 8 to 11) .... 1 plant
5. *Cotinus coggygria* Golden Spirit (syn. *C. coggygria* 'Ancot', smokebush, zones 5 to 8) .... 1 plant
6. *Dahlia* 'Bishop of Llandaff' (zones 8 to 11) .... 1 plant
7. *Ensete ventricosum* 'Maurelii' (banana, zones 9 to 11) 1 plant
8. *Eremurus* ×*isabellinus* 'Cleopatra' (foxtail lily, zones 5 to 8) .... 4 plants
9. *Euphorbia cotinifolia* (tropical smokebush, zones 10 to 11) .... 1 plant
10. *Euphorbia polychroma* 'Bonfire' (spurge, zones 5 to 9) .... 2 plants
11. *Hibiscus* 'Moy Grande' (zones 5 to 9) .... 1 plant
12. *Hypericum calycinum* 'Brigadoon' (St. John's wort, zones 5 to 7) .... 1 plant
13. *Kolkwitzia amabilis* Dream Catcher (syn. *K. amabilis* 'Maradco', beauty bush, zones 4 to 8) ...... 1 plant
14. *Lilium* 'Touching' (orienpet lily, zones 4 to 8) .... 6 plants
15. *Magnolia sieboldii* (Oyama magnolia, zones 5 to 8) ..... 1 plant
16. *Miscanthus sinensis* 'Gold Bar' (maiden grass, zones 5 to 9) .... 1 plant
17. *Miscanthus sinensis* 'Morning Light' (maiden grass, zones 5 to 9) .... 1 plant
18. *Rudbeckia hirta* 'Prairie Sun' (gloriosa daisy, zones 3 to 7) .... 2 plants
19. *Salvia guaranitica* 'Black and Blue' (sage, zones 7 to 10) .... 2 plants
20. *Wisteria frutescens* 'Amethyst Falls' (American wisteria, zones 5 to 9) .... 1 plant

Manihot esculenta 'Variegata'.

trouble with diseases and pests. Japanese beetles are especially attracted to them. Hibiscus may not be the first choice for deer, but the four-legged eating machines may take a nibble. If you would prefer to keep these plants around for a while, choose from among the loads of hybrids or the many hardy cultivars of the North American species *Hibiscus moscheutos* (zones 5 to 10).

Tapioca
Manihot species and cultivars, zones 8 to 11
Spring to fall (foliage)

Full sun to partial shade; moist, fertile soil

Even if it is not your favorite pudding flavor, tapioca will certainly win you over in the garden. This genus serves up unique tropical shrubs with deeply lobed foliage (roughly 8 inches wide) that complements patio, entryway, and container plantings. *Manihot esculenta* (zones 9 to 11) is the species responsible for that famous pudding (made from its roots). Do not go making the dessert from scratch yourself, however, unless you know what you are doing. The uncooked roots are poisonous. Roots aside, 'Variegata' (zones 10 to 11) is a sensational plant for its variegated leaves splashed with creamy yellow and its reddish pink leaf stalks. Averaging 3 to 8 feet tall and 3 to 5 feet wide, tapiocas can be used in small and large spaces. Like many tropical plants, they lean toward the smaller size of that range in the north, but they are also accepting of some shade in the south and are deer resistant. *Manihot grahamii* (zones 8 to 11), with intriguing wavy green leaflets, is another great choice. It is reported to be an aggressive self-sower that naturalizes in Gulf Coast states. This genus is relatively new in ornamental gardening arenas; do not be surprised to find a bit of variability in its reported hardiness zone range.

New Zealand flax
Phormium species and cultivars, zones 8 to 11
Spring to fall (foliage)

Full sun; moist, well-drained, fertile soil

For gardeners looking for something a little edgy, New Zealand flax is just the ticket. This fabulous tender perennial is reminiscent of hardy yucca (*Yucca filamentosa* and cultivars, zones 4 to 10), only it can get a little bigger and has more interesting leaves. Reaching up to 4 feet tall and wide in less temperate climates, New Zealand flax varieties offer swordlike leaves that vary in color from blue-green to bronze. *Phormium* 'Sundowner' and *P.* 'Carousel' are among the stars of the genus, featuring bronze-green leaves with apricot margins. New Zealand flaxes do not seem to flower during a short gardening season, but who cares? The foliage looks fantastic when paired with other bold and finely textured plants, and the wonderful warm tones combine handsomely with any color scheme. *Phormium tenax* (zones 8 to 11) is the most widely available species, while *P. cookianum* (zones 8 to 11) is a nice, typically smaller choice to keep an eye out for. These plants can be overwintered in an unheated garage, but it takes a month or two for them to really make a comeback in spring. No major pests or diseases seem to faze New Zealand flax. This bold beauty definitely deserves a gold star.

Phormium 'Carousel'. Taken at The New York Botanical Garden.

Castor bean

Ricinus communis and cultivars, zones 9 to 11
Spring to fall (foliage), summer to fall (seedpods)

Full sun; moist, fertile soil

It is often love at first sight when you see castor bean in the garden. The lush stand of large, deeply lobed leaves creates a mesmerizing 2- to 5-foot-wide backdrop on 4- to 10-foot-tall stems. The pleasing, green to rich, deep red foliage can get to be as wide as a large record album (for those of you who remember what those are), sometimes bigger. Plants with leaves with red undertones also exhibit the same wonderful color in their stems. The flowers are not all that exciting—small, yellowish, and open along a spike. 'Carmencita' and 'Carmencita Pink' seem to be the exception, with red and pink flowers, respectively. Both also feature beautiful, reddish bronze leaves. The seed capsules on all castor beans are a whole different story. The red, 1-inch-round, pointy spheres are fascinating and look kind of like a funky Christmas ornament. Conveniently enough, once the capsules dry the seeds can be easily collected and saved for sowing the next year. If small children or pets frequent your garden, pass on castor bean: all parts of this tropical shrub are poisonous. Otherwise, take advantage of their dramatic display and use them as a screen, foil, or focal point in sunny locations. Castor beans are rarely troubled by pests or diseases. If you can find it, 'Gibsonii' is a nice 4-foot-tall selection that works well in tight spaces.

Ricinus communis 'Carmencita Pink' before a backdrop of *Canna* 'Panache'. Courtesy of *Fine Gardening*, taken at Berkshire Botanical Garden.

ABUNDANT AND PLAYFUL

Thanks to lush, colorful annuals and tropicals, we have no shortage of beautiful flowers and foliage to enjoy in our favorite outdoor spaces throughout the summer months. Backyard dining areas, cozy hideaways, and welcoming entries are far more enticing when brimming with happy blooms and a swirl of tones, tints, hues, and textures. Many vivacious options provide generous, enchanting displays throughout the warmest months of the year. As with larger tropicals, these plants like a regular feeding either from a slow-release granular or water-soluble fertilizer. Providing them with a humus-rich bedding soil will typically carry them a long way.

Alternanthera

Alternanthera species and cultivars,
zones 10 to 11
Spring to summer (foliage)

Full sun to partial shade; consistently moist, well-drained, average soil

Alternantheras are excellent foliage plants that bring both attractive color and texture to the table. They are all quite diverse. *Alternanthera dentata* offers the cultivar 'Rubiginosa', which features deep burgundy-purple to almost black leaves that are 3 to 4 inches long. It stands 24 to 36 inches tall and about half as wide. *Alternanthera bettzichiana* is a low-growing (up to 12 inches tall and twice as wide) favorite for its unusual, party-colored foliage with shades of pink, green, yellow, and deep red-purple all appearing on each half-inch-long leaf. A third, widely available option is *A. fi-coidea*, which sports thin, almost needle-like, 1-inch-long leaves in burgundy ('Red Threads') or green and gold ('Gold Threads') tones. Its habit is similar to *A. bettzichiana*. In general these tender perennials make great edging plants. They welcome a little shade in hot climates and rarely have problems with pests or diseases.

Alternanthera ficoidea 'Red Threads' and *Plectranthus ciliatus* 'Drège'.

A Little Housekeeping Goes a Long Way

Everyone, including plants, needs a little spiffing up from time to time. In addition to basic light, water, and nutrition, a few snips of the pruners is all it takes to keep annuals and tropicals attractive and productive. Removing spent flowers, severely blemished leaves, and damaged shoots will instantly give plants a healthier appearance. Because it is a plant's mission in life to set seed and reproduce, deadheading most plants will also encourage more blooms. With true annuals, deadheading is imperative. If you let them set seed, they are done for. The good news is that many of the plants we call annuals are not true annuals. They are tropicals that cannot survive cold winters, and they keep right on trucking for the summer whether you remove the spent flowers or not.

Although it is not necessary, pinching plants with branching habits like coleus, lantana, or castor bean will encourage bushier, fuller growth. When you remove a tip of a stem it triggers side shoots to start sprouting. This technique will reduce the plant's overall size, keeping it more compact, but with the payoff of a lush appearance. Many times pinching can come in handy when you are trying to keep enthusiastic growers from overpowering a planting and its bedfellows. Once you get the hang of it, you

For bushier growth, pinch stem tips to the next set of leaves. Courtesy of Brent Benner.

will be amazed at how easy it is to manipulate a plant's growth and keep it in scale with smaller or slower-growing neighbors. All it takes is a simple snip of the stem.

Living to See Another Year

If it breaks your heart to throw tender tropicals in the compost pile at the end of the season, consider overwintering them indoors. For plants growing in containers, this just requires finding a good spot to place the pot. Plants sunk into the ground require a bit more effort because you have to lift and place them in a storage container. Many gardeners do not mind and often enjoy the challenge of keeping tropicals alive so that they can feature them in their

garden again. There are generally two types of indoor locations to choose from: warm and cool. Do not expect to bring true annuals in for the winter; they just do not have it in them to go another year.

If you have a warm (somewhere around 65°F) location near a sunny window, you can grow many tender gems in pots as houseplants—after all, traditional houseplants are tropicals. The plants may not look the greatest, but they will often live to see another year. Water them when the soil is dry and rotate the pots every week or two so that all sides of the plants have a turn in the brighter light. Expect leaves to drop and insects to hitch a ride indoors, especially whiteflies and aphids. Insects are difficult to avoid. Some gardeners like to do a preemptive strike before bringing plants indoors by spraying plants with insecticidal soap or other insect control. Insecticidal soap is highly regarded as a safe control and can even be made at home by adding 1 to 2 tablespoons of liquid castile soap to 1 gallon of water. If you find you have a large insect infestation after the plants are already indoors, you can knock down the numbers by treating them in the bathtub.

Many tender tropicals can also be overwintered in locations that maintain cool temperatures (around 40°F to 50°F) throughout the winter months. Places like basements or garages are good choices. The trick is to trigger your plants into dormancy, which is not done by exposure to cool temperatures but by dry conditions. A few weeks before you plan to bring these plants inside (before the first hard frost), cut off their water supply. When you bring them indoors, you can pretty much set them in a corner and forget about them until spring.

Some plants, like *Solenostemon scutellarioides* cultivars, can be easily grown from cuttings and overwintered near a sunny window.

Obviously this method will not work with all tropicals. It is particularly effective, however, with bulbous or fleshy-rooted plants like elephant's ears, which can be cut back to a few inches from the ground, gently lifted (shaking off excess soil), and stored in a shallow container. Overwintering is largely a trial-and-error venture; half the fun is seeing what you can get away with. When it comes time to bring your plants back outdoors, wait until the threat of frost has passed and slowly reintroduce them back to the sun. Start by placing them in full shade for the first week, then gradually move them into full sun.

More advanced gardeners overwinter plants by taking cuttings and investing in artificial indoor lighting to increase their holding area. High-intensity discharge (HID) lamps are the Cadillacs of lighting— relatively expensive but highly effective. Florescent lighting is a good inexpensive option that will get you by. Traditional shop lights purchased at a local home center and fitted with one warm-light (2700K to 3000K) tube and one cool-white (5000K and higher) tube will do the trick. You can also use the lights to start seeds indoors in late winter or early spring.

Angelonia

Angelonia angustifolia and cultivars, zones 9 to 11
Summer to fall (flowers)

Full sun; moist, well-drained, moderately fertile soil

Angelonia is a top-notch tender perennial that is a strong team player front-and-center or on the sidelines. Just pop it in place, stand back, and enjoy the show. This nonstop flowering machine produces 8- to 10-inch-tall spikes covered in white, pink, or purple blooms, depending on the selection. Plants typically stand 12 to 24 inches tall and 12 to 14 inches wide. They do not require deadheading, but occasional housekeeping will tidy things up a bit and encourage more blooms. Pinching stem tips will give plants a nice, bushy form. As a group, angelonias do not mind heat and will tolerate drier conditions, which makes them excellent substitutes for snapdragons (*Antirrhinum majus* cultivars, zones 7 to 10). They have few pest and disease foes and can easily be used throughout the garden to visually tie plantings together. Breeders have gone like gangbusters on this plant. The Angelface series is touted for its long, upright (nonfloppy) stems, while the Serena series offers more compact plants with a bushier form. There are many worthy plants to try. Angelonias are first-rate annuals; it is too bad they are not perennial.

Angelonia Angelface Pink (syn. *Angelonia* 'Anpink', bottom left) with *Salvia* cultivars (top left and right), *Euphorbia marginata* (top center), an *Iris* cultivar (center), and a *Verbena* cultivar (bottom right). Taken at Linden Hill Gardens.

Caladium

Caladium species and cultivars, zones 10 to 11
Spring to fall (foliage)

Partial to full shade; moist, well-drained, fertile soil

One look at these leaves and you might conclude that Mother Nature, Georgia O'Keeffe, and Jackson Pollock were in the same art class together. Caladium dazzles the eye with big expanses of color as well as wonderful streaks and splotches. Few shade plants can match these beauties when it comes to livening up the garden. The elongated, heart-shaped leaves are 6 to 12 inches long and held on 8- to 24-inch-tall stems. *Caladium* 'Candidum' glows with white leaves and striking green veining, while *C.* 'Gingerland' provides an engaging display of cranberry splatters over splashes of green and white. This tropical perennial likes humidity but can sometimes suffer from rot and diseases if too wet. Deer are not completely opposed to giving it a try.

Caladium usually works best as the center of attention. The wonderful green, red, white, or pink hues of the leaves provide lots of opportunities to create interesting color echoes in planting designs. Their wild patterns and colors are definitely for the gardener who likes to shake things up.

Caladium 'Gingerland'.

Impatiens Fusion Heat skirts the base of *Caladium* 'Gingerland' and a *Solenostemon scutellarioides* cultivar as *Dichondra argentea* 'Silver Falls' spills over the edge of this container. Taken at the Benner Garden.

Impatiens

Impatiens species and cultivars, zones 10 to 11
Summer to fall (flowers)

Partial to full shade; moist, well-drained, fertile soil

They may not be the rock stars of the plant world, but impatiens earn their keep in the garden. This large group of annuals and tropical perennials reliably provides loads of cheery blooms in shady nooks and crannies. They do not require deadheading but can easily be pinched back to encourage more flowering lateral shoots. Traditional species like *Impatiens walleriana* (zones 10 to 11), and its cultivars, can be anywhere from 6 to 30 inches tall and 6 to 24 inches wide with flat, disklike flowers that are 1 to 2 inches wide, while hybrids in the New Guinea group (syn. *I. hawkeri* cultivars) tend to hover around a foot tall and wide. Options in shades of pink, purple, red, orange, yellow, and white are all easy to find. Some double-flowering varieties are also available, as are unique cup- or seashell-shaped selections. The Fusion series displays this unusual cup shape in shades of salmon and orange.

Impatiens love heat and humidity and are true workhorse plants. They are occasionally eaten by deer and may have run-ins with insects or diseases, such as spider mites or leaf spot—no serious problems worth banning them from the garden, however.

Lantana

Lantana camara cultivars, zones 8 to 11
Summer to fall (flowers)

Full sun; moderately moist, well-drained, average soil

Lantana 'Athens Rose'.

Although considered a tropical shrub weed in temperate climates where it is hardy, lantana is a choice tender selection in cooler regions. This plant just loves to bloom. The festive, often multicolored, clustered flowers grow to about the size of a quarter. They often come in shades of red, orange, pink, lavender, or white mixed with yellow. 'Athens Rose' is a pleasing mix of yellow and pink petals that makes you think of yellow and pink lemonade. Luscious Grape (syn. 'Robpwpur') has pink-purple blossoms with white centers. 'Samantha' has wonderful yellow variegation on its leaves that is mirrored by a lovely yellow flower.

In its exotic, native habitat, lantana can reach up to 6 feet tall and wide; it typically grows 2 to 3 feet tall and wide when cultivated as an annual. Some selections are more trailing, while others are upright. The medium green leaves have a wonderful, wrinkly, almost leathery texture and can be variegated. Lantana fills in quickly and combines well with other plants at the front and middle of the border or in containers. It is a butterfly magnet and has no serious pest or disease problems. However, it is a noxious weed in a handful of temperate locales, so check your state invasive listings. Most cultivars will continue to flower without deadheading. If the variety you choose appears to produce copious amounts of tiny, peasize seedpods, however, deadheading to encourage more blooms is not a bad idea. Watch out if you have a strong sniffer—some folks find the scent of lantana unpleasant.

Pentas lanceolata Starla Pink. Courtesy of *Fine Gardening*.

Pentas

Pentas lanceolata and cultivars, zones 9 to 11
Summer to fall (flowers)

Full sun; moist, well-drained, fertile soil

This happy-go-lucky plant fits in well with any sunny planting scheme. Considered a shrubby perennial in its native Africa, pentas works as a stellar annual in nontropical climates. The clusters of star-shaped flowers are the perfect landing pads for butterflies and are also well liked by hummingbirds. Cultivars and hybrids with blooms in shades of red, pink, lilac, and white are widely available. Handsome green, fuzzy leaves set the flowers off sublimely. Depending on the variety, plants can reach 14 to 36 inches tall and wide. Pentas may be occasionally visited by aphids and spider mites, but deer do not seem to be interested in it. Plants benefit from an occasional deadheading. Pentas pairs well with other annuals, perennials, summer bulbs, and woody plants. There is a deluge of cultivars out there that probably only breeders can tell apart. The New Look series offers vigorous seed-propagated plants. The Butterfly series is loaded with strong performers. The biggest deviant from this vast group is 'Stars and Stripes', which has distinct variegated leaves accompanied by red blooms. Otherwise, choose whatever flower color and plant size strike your fancy at the garden center. The odds are pretty good you will get a top-notch selection.

Coleus

Solenostemon scutellarioides cultivars,
zones 10 to 11
Spring to fall (foliage)

Full sun to partial shade; moist, well-drained,
fertile soil

If there is one tender perennial that no
garden should be without, it is coleus.
It grows in sun or shade, and although
its flowers are insignificant, its foliage is
phenomenal. Hundreds of cultivars are
available, with colors that span the spectrum. The options really are endless, from
wild and garish to simple and subtle. The
size and shape of the leaves are also quite
variable. You can choose varieties with foliage that is thin and gently scalloped or
wide and heavily serrated, depending on
your mood. Coleus can be cast as the star
of the show or a supporting character. It
plays very nicely with others. Selections
with large, solid-colored leaves like the
aptly named 'Orange King' (syn. 'Gold
Giant') are especially easy to work with,
going with practically anything, while
multicolored, fine-textured varieties like
'Kiwi Fern' may take a bit more thought
to find complementary companions. Coleus can grow up 3 feet tall and wide. Some
varieties have a more upright habit,
while others tend to be more spreading,
even trailing. These plants respond well
to pruning and can easily be pinched and
snipped to encourage bushier growth
and a more compact form. They can also
be trained into standards. Most people
remove the flowers to direct energy into
the leaves. Coleus is rarely troubled by
pests or diseases. Deer may give it a try,
but beyond that, it could seriously be the
perfect annual.

Solenostemon scutellarioides 'Orange King' (syn. *S. scutellarioides* 'Gold Giant').

Torenia Catalina Midnight Blue (syn. *T.* 'Dancat911').

Wishbone flower
Torenia fournieri cultivars, annual
Summer to fall (flowers)

Partial to full shade; moist, well-drained, fertile soil

Wishbone flower does not look like much when sitting in a tiny pot on a bench at the garden center. Once you try it, however, it will become a permanent part of your garden roster. This enthusiastic bloomer produces white, pink, purple, blue, or yellow flowers that typically feature white throats and yellow or more deeply toned markings. The flowers are 1 to 2 inches long and do not require deadheading. This true annual gets its common name from the two tiny anthers that form in each flower and resemble a wishbone. Plants grow up to 12 inches tall and sometimes just as wide. Their mounding, trailing habit makes them ideal for the front of a bed or edging in containers. The Moon series offers a great spectrum of colors, including various yellows and magenta. The Catalina series also offers a good mix of color options. Wishbone flower tends to like it on the cooler side. It performs best in full shade in hot, humid climates. Otherwise, it does not have any serious foes. If you have had trouble with this plant in the past, perhaps try a selection from the Summer Wave series, which was bred to hold up better under hot, humid conditions. While *Torenia fournieri* seems to be the most widely cultivated species, many of the varieties available are considered hybrids.

Cool Annuals

Although they may not survive severe winter temperatures, some annuals prefer cool temperatures. Gardeners with mild winters can enjoy many of these plants during the winter months. Many are cold hardy in warmer zones, but it is often summer heat and humidity that do these plants in. Cool-season annuals and tender perennials can be grown throughout the summer in areas that experience cooler temperatures, such as places with higher altitudes or near a coastline. They can also be put to good use in spring to provide a burst of color while you are waiting to put out your heat-loving plants. The following options will work well in a mostly sunny location.

Antirrhinum majus **cultivars** (snapdragon, zones 7 to 10)
Calendula officinalis **and cultivars** (pot marigold, annual)
Diascia **species and cultivars** (twinspur, zones 7 to 10)
Gerbera jamesonii **and cultivars** (Gerbera daisy, zones 8 to 11)
Lathyrus odoratus **and cultivars** (sweet pea, annual)
Lobularia maritima **and cultivars** (sweet alyssum, annual)
Matthiola incana **and cultivars** (stock, zones 6 to 8)
Nemesia strumosa **and cultivars** (annual)
Osteospermum **species and cultivars** (Cape daisy, zones 10 to 11)
Viola ×wittrockiana **cultivars** (pansy, zones 6 to 10)

1. *Antirrhinum majus* 'Rocket Pink'.

2. *Lobularia maritima* 'Snow Crystals'.

Okay, never say never, but self-sowing annuals or short-lived tender perennials are great for fairly reliable, serendipitous displays each year. Once you plant them and let them set seed, they will happily spread their progeny about. The kids may not pop up in the exact same place, but that is what makes this gardening adventure fun. The newbies create all sorts of unexpected combinations and surprises when they sprout each year. They are also pretty easy to pluck out of the garden if you do not like how things are going. Some plants are more prolific than others, such as tall verbena (*Verbena bonariensis*). If you are not absolutely in love with the plant, do not let it go to seed. Ask other gardeners in your area how intensely particular plants seed before planting them in your garden, and always check to see if a plant is listed as invasive in your area before welcoming it into the fold.

Centaurea cyanus **and cultivars** (bachelor's buttons, annual)

Cosmos bipinnatus **and cultivars** (annual)

Dianthus barbatus **and cultivars** (sweet William, zones 3 to 9, biennial)

Eschscholzia californica **and cultivars** (California poppy, annual)

Impatiens balsamina **and cultivars** (balsam, annual)

Linum grandiflorum **and cultivars** (flowering flax, annual)

Nicotiana **species and cultivars** (flowering tobacco, zones 10 to 11)

Nigella damascena **and cultivars** (love-in-a-mist, annual)

Rudbeckia hirta **and cultivars** (gloriosa daisy, zones 3 to 7)

Verbena bonariensis (tall verbena, zones 7 to 11)

1. *Rudbeckia hirta* 'Indian Summer'.

2. *Verbena bonariensis.* Taken at The New York Botanical Garden.

7 Edibles

Ornamental vegetables and herbs are the ultimate multifunctional plants, offering food and beauty. Even though many of these gems have been historically grown in crop rows or individual plots, they are right at home in the mixed border, rubbing elbows with your favorite annuals, perennials, bulbs, trees, and shrubs.

Edible plants can be a feast for the eyes, too. Plants like *Beta vulgaris* 'Bull's Blood' (left of center), *Allium schoenoprasum* var. *sibiricum* (top right), and *Salvia officinalis* 'Purpurascens' (bottom) fit right in with ornamental *Zinnia* and *Salvia* cultivars (top left). Taken at Cornell Plantations.

Allium schoenoprasum.

While some ornamental edibles are perennial, many are not hardy and are grown as annuals. The key to success is to pair them with other plants that have similar light, water, and soil requirements. Many of these veggies and herbs also make great container plants. Placing them in pots allows you to bring them right up on your deck or patio, where they are easy to harvest.

AROMATIC HERBS

Caution: Brushing up against these plants or handling their leaves might make your tummy grumble. Many aromatic edibles are the herbs we enjoy in our favorite foods. They are useful beyond taste, however, providing striking foliage and flowers. Species with gray-green or purple-tinged foliage are especially useful when creating captivating combinations. These tones provide a pleasing backdrop for more colorful plants and can be used as a common thread to visually sew plantings together.

Chives

Allium schoenoprasum and cultivars, zones 3 to 9
Spring to summer (flowers)

Full sun to partial shade; moderately moist, well-drained, fertile soil

Chives is often a gardener's first introduction to the wonderful world of *Allium*. It is a big seller in the herb section of the garden center, used to flavor salads, soups, vinegars, and anything else you would like to enhance with a mild onion taste. Chives are a great addition to the mixed border. Their grasslike leaves form a robust clump that grows up to

24 inches tall and about half as wide. The 1-inch-round flowers appear in late spring or early summer and resemble small, lavender pompons. The several cultivars available display very subtle differences from the top-notch species. The biggest variation is the bloom color, which strays from the traditional pale purple shades to produce pink or white flowers. Seek out 'Corsican White' if you want a white variety. 'Forescate' offers nice, rosy red blooms. No matter the color, both the blossoms and leaves can be used in favorite dishes. Thankfully, deer do not find chives palatable, and plants are not plagued by any other pests or diseases. In fact, chives are sometimes planted around leafy vegetables to serve as an insect deterrent.

Fennel

Foeniculum vulgare and cultivars, zones 6 to 9
Spring to fall (foliage), summer (flowers)

Full sun; moist, well-drained, fertile soil

Fennel has been gracing gardens as an ornamental perennial and culinary herb for years. Its wonderful, lacy leaves expand up to 12 inches long, offering a fine texture that is fun to play with in bed and border planting schemes. In the kitchen, cooks use everything from the anise-flavored-and-scented leaves to the stems to the seeds in salads, soups, sauces, and breads. Plants can grow 4 to 6 feet tall and 2 feet wide. Tiny, yellow umbel flowers appear during the second half of summer. If allowed to go to seed, fennel will freely self-sow, providing more flavor for the next gardening season. It is not bothered by diseases but can be visited by a few insect pests. The leaves and stems pack too much flavor for deer but are a favorite among swallowtail caterpillars. Many gardeners plant fennel just to attract butterflies. Plants can be inclined to bolt during the maximum heat of summer. Cultivars with deep bronze leaves like 'Purpureum' and 'Smokey' are particularly attractive in mixed plantings and containers. The blue-green foliage and stems of the straight species is also quite fetching, especially as it sends out its reddish-tinged new growth.

Foeniculum vulgare. Courtesy of *Fine Gardening.*

Lavandula angustifolia 'Hidcote'. Taken at Cornell Plantations.

Lavender

Lavandula species and cultivars, zones 5 to 10
Spring to fall (foliage), summer (flowers)

Full sun; dry to adequately moist, sharp-draining, moderately fertile soil

What gardener does not swoon at the sight and smell of lavender in full bloom? Whole festivals are devoted to this enchanting herb. You can even find its soothing scent in hand soap and fabric softener. Lavender's fragrant, linear leaves appear on 12- to 36-inch-tall stems. Some species can grow more than 36 inches wide, but most produce a 24- to 30-inch spread. With summer comes an abundantly delightful display of, you guessed it, lavender-purple spikes that measure 2 to 6 inches in length. Select cultivars also offer blooms in shades of white, pink, and even a touch of red. *Lavandula angustifolia* 'Hidcote' (zones 5 to 9) is a good all-around, purple-flowering choice, while *L. angustifolia* 'Rosea' (syn. *L. angustifolia* 'Jean Davis', zones 5 to 9) has pale pink blooms, and *L.* ×*intermedia* 'Alba' (syn. *L.* 'Alba', zones 6 to 9) is a nice white-flowering option.

Although some growers claim that certain selections are cold hardy in zone 5 and heat hardy in zone 10, these designations can be hit or miss. Few pests and diseases bother with lavender, including deer. It is usually drainage that does this plant in. Sharp drainage, especially in winter, is a must. Many gardeners who do not have the right drainage are content to grow this tantalizing herb as an annual. Pruning too early in the spring can also impair your plant. Wait until new growth has started and the threat of frost has passed.

Believe it or not, you can eat lavender, which can be found in cookies and ice cream at gourmet shops. These sweet treats are not bad if you can get past eating something that smells like soap.

Monarda 'Raspberry Wine'.

Bee balm

Monarda didyma and cultivars, zones 3 to 9
Summer (flowers)

Full sun to partial shade; moist to wet, well-drained, fertile soil

When bee balm is in bloom at the nursery, it usually finds its way into your car. The cheery, red, pink, purple, or white blossoms appear in a unique 2-inch-wide cluster that looks like some type of summertime whirligig. The flowers are a hit with hummingbirds and butterflies as they stand on 36-inch-tall stems that form a 24-inch-wide clump. This North American native is good for naturalizing and will continue to bloom with deadheading. It tends to perform better in the cooler end of its zone range. Problems with the yearly return of powdery mildew have turned many gardeners off of this perennial herb. Choosing disease-resistant varieties (usually hybrids),

giving plants plenty of elbow room for air circulation, and avoiding wet leaves at night will help alleviate the problem. The flowers pack a punch even from a distance. If you keep bee balm on the sidelines, in a less prominent place, any mildew issues that do creep up will not cause much of a visual disturbance. Mildew aside, bee balm is an easygoing, deer-resistant plant that does not mind a little afternoon shade. Its flowers and citrusy, ovate leaves are often used in teas. 'Jacob Cline', 'Marshall's Delight', and 'Raspberry Wine' are good, fairly mildew-resistant choices to start with.

Scented Segue

Creating a welcoming swirl of pleasing fragrances when you are typically outdoors the most, from spring to fall, is a great way to heighten interest in a sunny location. The best place to put fragrant plants is where you walk and linger most often. It is always a joy to return home and walk up a scented path. Weaving shrubs and grasses into your design offers structure and additional interest throughout the year, while a mix of soft pastel colors sets the stage for a delightful, soothing interlude before going into the house.

Plant List

1. *Brugmansia* 'Pink Beauty'
   (angel's trumpet, zones 9 to 11) .... 1 plant

2. *Buddleja* 'Pink Delight' (butterfly bush, zones 5 to 9) . 1 plant

3. *Calamintha nepeta* subsp. *nepeta*
   (syn. *C. nepetoides*, calamint, zones 5 to 8) .... 9 plants

4. *Caryopteris* ×*clandonensis* 'Longwood Blue'
   (bluebeard, zones 5 to 9) .... 1 plant

5. *Caryopteris* ×*clandonensis* 'Summer Sorbet'
   (bluebeard, zones 5 to 8) .... 1 plant

6. *Clethra alnifolia* 'Ruby Spice'
   (summersweet, zones 4 to 9) .... 1 plant

7. *Daphne* ×*burkwoodii* 'Carol Mackie' (zones 4 to 8) 1 plant

8. *Echinacea purpurea* 'White Swan'
   (coneflower, zones 3 to 8) .... 2 plants

9. *Echinacea* 'Sunrise'
   (Big Sky series, coneflower, zones 4 to 9) .... 2 plants

10. *Heliotropium arborescens* 'Marine'
    (heliotrope, zones 10 to 11) .... 5 plants

11. *Hemerocallis* 'Happy Returns' (daylily, zones 3 to 9) 5 plants

12. *Iris pallida* 'Argentea Variegata'
    (variegated sweet iris, zones 4 to 9) .... 4 plants

13. *Lablab purpureus* (hyacinth bean, zones 9 to 11) .... 1 plant

14. *Lavandula angustifolia* 'Hidcote Pink'
    (English lavender, zones 5 to 9) .... 2 plants

15. *Lavandula angustifolia* 'Munstead'
    (English lavender, zones 5 to 9) .... 2 plants

16. *Lilium* 'Casa Blanca' (lily, zones 5 to 8) .... 6 plants

17. *Lilium* 'Star Gazer' (lily, zones 3 to 8) .... 9 plants

18. *Nicotiana* ×*sanderae* Sensation Pink
    (flowering tobacco, zones 10 to 11) .... 7 plants

19. *Nicotiana sylvestris* (flowering tobacco, zones 10 to 11) 7 plants

20. *Paeonia* 'Etched Salmon' (peony, zones 3 to 7) .... 1 plant

21. *Paeonia* 'Miss America' (peony, zones 3 to 7) .... 1 plant

22. *Philadelphus* 'Snow Dwarf'
    (mockorange, zones 4 to 8) .... 1 plant

23. *Rosa* Pink Knock Out
    (syn. *R.* 'Radcon', rose, zones 5 to 9) .... 1 plant

24. *Syringa pubescens* subsp. *patula* 'Miss Kim'
    (lilac, zones 3 to 8) .... 1 plant

Planting Plan

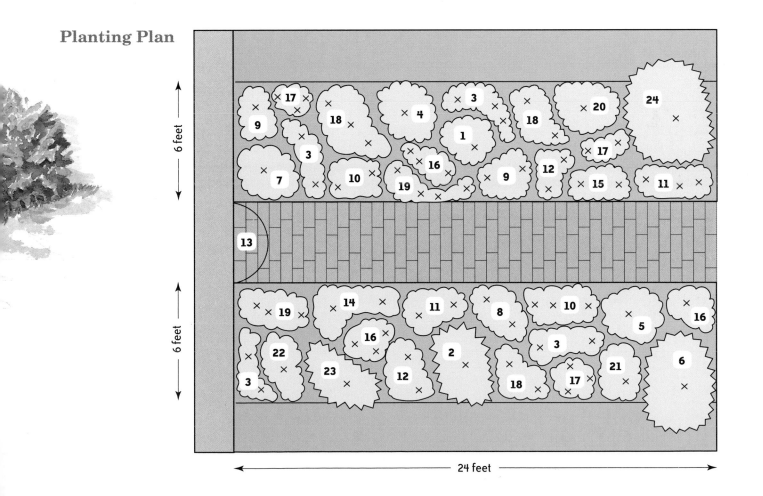

Ocimum 'African Blue' (left) with *Nicotiana* 'Lime Green' (top), a *Cosmos* cultivar (right), and an *Ageratum* cultivar (bottom). Taken at Berkshire Botanical Garden.

Basil

Ocimum species and cultivars, zones 9 to 11
Summer to fall (foliage), summer (flowers)

Full sun; moist, well-drained, somewhat lean soil

Basil is another herb that delivers two benefits for the price of one: flavor and looks. You would be hard-pressed to find a person unfamiliar with this plant's culinary uses. Pesto is a particularly well known application, but the 2-inch-long, elliptic leaves are also used around the world to flavor everything from vinegar to ice cream. Each basil selection offers a taste all its own. Several have dark purple leaves, like *Ocimum basilicum* var. *purpurascens* 'Purple Ruffles', or green-and-white variegated foliage, like *O. ×citriodorum* 'Pesto Perpetuo'. Although most gardeners growing basil for the table try to keep the white, pink, or purple flowers from developing (to encourage leaf production), a number of varieties, like *O.* 'African Blue', feature very handsome blooms. Some basils are considered tropical perennials, but as a whole they are widely grown as annuals. Plants can experience an occasional visit from less desirable garden inhabitants such as Japanese beetles, aphids, slugs, and cutworms. On the flip side, basil reportedly repels mosquitoes. Periodic fungal diseases and rot may occur, which are primarily triggered by overwatering and wet leaves. The good news is that deer do not like basil, and its benefits far outweigh any minor negatives. You can count on this heat-loving plant to fill the garden and kitchen with lots of flavor throughout the gardening season.

Rosemary

Rosmarinus officinalis and cultivars, zones 6 to 11
Spring to fall (foliage), spring to summer (flowers)

Full sun; dry to moist, well-drained, lean to average soil

This culinary herb may kick it up a notch in the kitchen, but it also pulls its weight in the garden. Where it is hardy, rosemary grows into a handsome, upright, 4- to 6-foot-tall shrub that is almost equally wide. Otherwise it is grown as a smaller annual herb and is sometimes brought indoors over winter with mixed success. Rosemary's silvery green, needlelike leaves are about 2 inches long and have an enchanting scent and a delicious flavor that is used to enhance all sorts of cuisines. Small, blue, sometimes white or pink, flowers appear in the leaf axils at the tips of the branches. In cooler regions the bloom occurs in spring or early summer. In the southern United States the flowers appear much earlier. A great many cultivars offer variations on flower color, foliage size and color, and habit. Low-growing, creeping varieties like 'Huntington Carpet' (zones 7 to 10) spill nicely over the edge of a container or retaining wall. 'Arp' (zones 6 to 10) is one of the more hardy varieties. 'Majorca Pink' (zones 7 to 10) has nice pink blooms. Rosemary has few run-ins with pests and diseases. It can have fungal problems in humid areas. As with other aromatic herbs, deer do not find this plant appealing.

Rosmarinus officinalis. Courtesy of *Fine Gardening*, taken at the United States National Arboretum.

Salvia officinalis 'Berggarten'.

Sage

Salvia officinalis and cultivars, zones 4 to 8
Spring to fall (foliage), summer (flowers)

Full sun; dry to moderately moist, sharp-draining, fertile soil

Unlike the vast majority of the *Salvia* brood, this common sage is all about the foliage, not the flowers. The 3-inch-long leaves have been used to flavor food for centuries, while their woolly texture performs as the perfect garden foil. The foliage has a wonderful blue-green tone, but selections like 'Icterina' boast yellow to creamy white variegation, and 'Purpurascens' offers a nice purple-tinged overlay. This perennial species has a mounding form that stands 12 to 36 inches tall with an 18- to 36-inch spread, depending on the cultivar. Sage looks great tumbling over the edge of a walkway, patio planter, or raised bed. 'Berggarten' is a great choice in any location where it can show off its larger-than-normal leaves. Sages do produce small, attractive, lavender-blue flower spikes in early summer, but the display is not nearly as impressive as the show given by the many other ornamental members of this genus. No serious pests or diseases harass this species. As with lavender, however, it does require sharp drainage.

Thyme

Thymus species and cultivars, zones 4 to 10
Spring to fall (foliage), summer (flowers)

Full sun; dry to moderately moist, sharp-draining, gritty soil

Thyme is another great little bed edger. This genus offers well more than 350 species with predominantly low-growing habits that reach 2 to 16 inches tall and 8 to 18 inches wide. The tiny, fragrant leaves grow to about the size of your pinky fingernail. Several species, including lemon thyme (*Thymus citriodorus*, zones 5 to 9) and common thyme (*T. vulgaris*, zones 5 to 9), also offer a wonderful flavor that is often relished in the kitchen. Depending on the variety, the leaves can be medium green, yellow, or variegated with white or yellow margins. *Thymus pulegioides* 'Bertram Anderson' (syn. *T.* 'Anderson's Gold', zones 4 to 9) is a great golden thyme, while *T. citriodorus* 'Argenteus' (zones 5 to 9) is an especially popular variegated selection with thin white margins around each leaf. Most thymes are cloaked with small but abundant lavender, pink, or white blooms for several weeks during summer. They are rarely troubled by pests or diseases. Low or mat-forming selections like woolly thyme (*T. pseudolanuginosus*, zones 5 to 8) grow especially well in crevices in walkways and patios. As with many woody-stemmed herbs, thyme should only be pruned after the growth is well on its way in spring, and never deep into its woody branches.

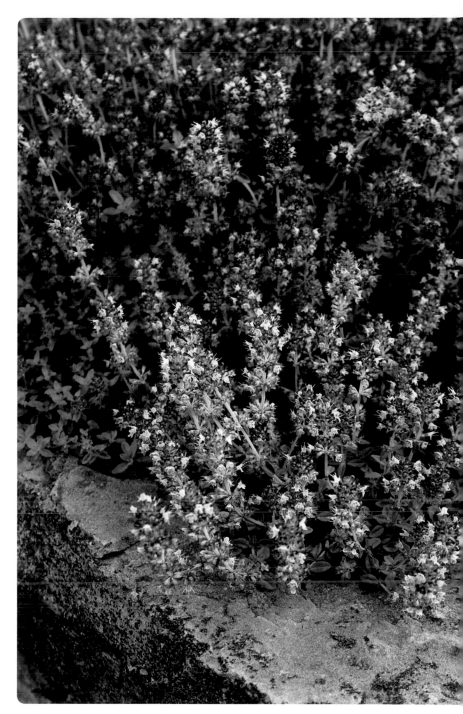

Thymus 'Creeping Lemon'.

Inferno Strip

You may not be ready to give up your front lawn, but perhaps you are ready to give up that ugly, hard-to-maintain strip along the road, sidewalk, or driveway often called a parking strip or hellstrip. Choosing a mix of colorful, tough, drought-tolerant plants to go in these hot, sunny locations beats the heck out of brown, dried-out grass in the summer. Take special care to select low-growing plants so that you can see children playing, bicycles passing by, and oncoming traffic. If your strip is along a parking area, include a few spots with stepping-stones to give drivers and passengers a place to step when exiting their cars.

Plant List

1. *Achillea* 'Moonshine' (yarrow, zones 3 to 8) .... 4 plants
2. *Artemisia* 'Powis Castle' (zones 6 to 9) .... 2 plants
3. *Delosperma* Mesa Verde (syn. *D.* 'Kelaidis', ice plant, zones 5 to 8) ... 2 plants
4. *Kniphofia hirsuta* 'Fire Dance' (red hot poker, zones 5 to 8) .... 2 plants
5. *Lantana* 'Athens Rose' (zones 8 to 11) .... 6 plants
6. *Linum perenne* 'Appar' (blue flax, zones 3 to 9) .... 4 plants
7. *Oenothera fremontii* 'Shimmer' (evening primrose, zones 4 to 8) ... 3 plants
8. *Stachys* 'Hidalgo' (betony, zones 7 to 9) .... 3 plants
9. *Stipa tenuissima* (syn. *Nassella tenuissima*, Mexican feather grass, zones 7 to 11) .... 5 plants
10. *Thymus vulgaris* 'Orange Balsam' (common thyme, zones 5 to 9) ... 3 plants

Planting Plan

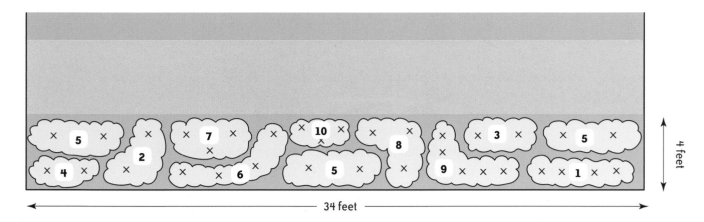

Beta vulgaris 'Ruby Red'.

PALATABLE BEAUTIES

While lettuces and peppers may not be the first plants that to come to mind when you hear the phrase "ornamental edibles," they will quickly become part of your yearly garden menu once you see them in action. They are among the many palatable choices that offer attractive foliage, interesting flowers, or colorful fruit. These plants work well along bed edges. Some prefer cooler temperatures, which works out well since options can be limited during cool seasons. As with many of the aromatic herbs, these more traditional kitchen garden plants combine well with other ornamental favorites, creating dynamic textural vignettes.

Sugar beet

Beta vulgaris and cultivars, biennial
Spring to summer (foliage)

Full sun to partial shade; moist, well-drained, fertile soil

If you are confused by this species, you are not alone. It seems to be two plants crammed into one name. Straight-up *Beta vulgaris* is good old sugar beet, but tack on a few convoluted ranks and you have yourself Swiss chard, *B. vulgaris* subsp. *cicla* var. *flavescens*. Names aside, these plants produce fabulous foliage that will knock your socks off when combined with ornamentals in the garden. Sugar beet cultivars like 'Bull's Blood' create drama with their dramatic deep red foliage. Swiss chard is also great for making a splash with its puckered texture and bright stalks. The stalks are

usually red but can come in a rainbow of colors that also show up in the leaf veins. The aptly named 'Bright Lights' offers vibrant yellow, orange, pink, or purple stalks. The narrow foliage of sugar beet and Swiss chard can reach 8 to 12 inches long if you let it—many gardeners like to eat the leaves. The foliage is susceptible to insects like leafminers. Deer may also take a liking to the leaves. Plants typically range from 12 to 24 inches tall and maybe half as wide. This species is a cool-season biennial that is grown as an annual. Swiss chard can sometimes take the summer heat, however, and last into autumn.

Kale

Brassica oleracea cultivars, zones 7 to 11
Spring and fall (foliage)

Full sun; moist, well-drained, fertile soil

Although this species is just as confusing as *Beta vulgaris*, it does offer some excellent cool-season foliage plants. While broccoli, cauliflower, cabbage, and Brussels sprouts all go by the name *Brassica oleracea*, kale (also known as ornamental cabbage) varieties are an excellent choice for the nonstop garden. Kales shine during the cooler times of year and can last into midsummer and beyond in regions with less heat and humidity. Gardeners in other areas can try to extend the show by planting their kales in partial shade. These plants are typically grown as annuals in spring and autumn. The leaves are quite variable in shape and color. Depending on the cultivar, some kales have long, narrow, blue-green leaves like 'Nero di Toscana' (syn. 'Lacinato'), while others have deeply cut leaves in shades of white, purple, or pink, such as 'Red Peacock'. The leaves can grow up to a foot long on plants that stand 12 to 36 inches tall and slightly less wide, which makes kale a good choice for the front or middle of the border and at the base of taller plants. The foliage is susceptible to insect and deer damage. Usually by the time anything totally ravages them, you are ready to yank the plants out anyway. Like the rest of the members of this species, kale is edible. Many cooks enjoy sautéing the young leaves, which are rich in vitamins.

Brassica oleracea 'Red Peacock'.

Battling Bugs

Unless you count those made of plastic, no plants live insect free. Creepy-crawly bugs are an important part of gardening. They are key members of our gardening crew, building soil, pollinating flowers, and wiping out bad guys. If you see one you do not like, do not be too quick to squash it. Figure out which insect you have and its role in the garden (and beyond) before you go hosing everything down with pesticide. Even if it is doing damage, you could be annihilating the larvae of a precious butterfly or predatory beneficials like praying mantis and ladybugs. Also weigh whether the damage the insect is doing really warrants action. Is it threatening the plant's health or just making it look bad for a little while? Is it worth the risk of exposing toxins to you, your family, your pets, or beneficial insects? Learning to tolerate some damage is good for the health of your garden and the environment. If you are not sure what you have, your local Cooperative Extension office can help you figure it out.

If you do decide to take action, consider using more environmentally friendly methods instead of reaching for toxic chemicals like those containing carbaryl (brand name Sevin). With each passing year, more and more earth-safe options are offered at garden centers, and entire online stores are devoted to low-impact pest management. You can purchase and release predatory beneficial insects. Many biologically based products are available, which are less hazardous to humans and wildlife. Neem oil, for example, is derived from neem tree seed. The active ingredients azadirachtin and clarified hydrophobic extract effectively control a number of insect pests and help with the management of some fungal diseases, respectively. Likewise, insecticidal soap puts fatty acid salts into action to control insects like aphids and mealy bugs. Before using any pest control product, always read the label to make sure your target is appropriate and that you understand how to safely apply it.

It is okay to have chomped leaves. Plants like milkweed (*Asclepias* species and cultivars) fortify monarch caterpillars so that they can turn into beautiful butterflies. Taken at the Brine Garden.

Of course, taking steps to prevent damaging insect infestations is always the most earth-friendly tactic. Plants are most susceptible when under stress. Be sure they are receiving optimum light, water, and nutrients as well as adequate drainage. Choosing pest-resistant varieties minimizes occurrences. You can also experiment with companion planting. Some research has found that aromatic plants like chives, basil, lemon thyme, and nasturtium repel insects. Similarly, strategically placing a mix of flowering and native plants will attract beneficial insects and give them a reason to stick around after they have reduced the number of bad guys.

Flowers You Can Eat

It may seem strange, but many flowers are edible. Their flavors can range from mild like a lettuce to spicy like a pepper. Flowers can be used as a dinner plate garnish, mixed in with salads, and decoratively placed on desserts. The best time to harvest them is when they are at their peak and in the morning after any dew has dried. Pollen can affect the flavor, so remove the stamens and pistils. Gently rinse your flowers to clean off any soil or insects; then lightly pat them dry with a kitchen towel or paper towel. If you do not plan to use the blooms right away, harvest them with their stems and keep them in a container of water. Small flowers can be kept for a few hours in a plastic bag with a moist paper towel (for humidity) in the refrigerator. The next time you are looking to perk up a dish, go out to the garden and see if any of the following edible blossoms (including their cultivars) are in bloom. (Make sure to avoid consuming flowers that have been treated with pesticide, however; if you are not sure whether they have been treated, don't eat them.)

Agastache foeniculum (anise hyssop, zones 3 to 9)
Alcea rosea (hollyhock, zones 3 to 9)
Allium schoenoprasum (chives, zones 3 to 9)
Anethum graveolens (dill, annual)
Calendula officinalis (pot marigold, annual)
Centaurea cyanus (bachelor's buttons, annual)
Chamaemelum nobile (chamomile, zones 4 to 9)
Dianthus species (zones 3 to 10)
Foeniculum vulgare (fennel, zones 6 to 9)
Hemerocallis species (daylily, zones 3 to 10)
Hibiscus rosa-sinensis (zones 9 to 11)
Lavandula species (lavender, zones 5 to 10)
Monarda didyma (bee balm, zones 3 to 9)
Ocimum basilicum (basil, zones 9 to 11)
Pelargonium species (scented geranium, zones 10 to 11)
Phaseolus coccineus (runner bean, zones 10 to 11)
Rosmarinus officinalis (rosemary, zones 6 to 11)
Salvia officinalis (sage, zones 4 to 8)
Thymus species (thyme, zones 4 to 10)
Tropaeolum majus (nasturtium, zone 11)
Tulipa species (tulip, zones 3 to 8)
Viola tricolor (Johnny-jump-up, annual)

1. *Anethum graveolens.*

2. *Tulipa* 'Bleu Aimable'.

Capsicum annuum
'Black Pearl'.

Pepper
Capsicum annuum cultivars, zones 9 to 11
Summer (fruit, foliage)

Full sun; consistently moist, well-drained, fertile soil

Peppers do a bang-up job of spicing it up in not only the kitchen but also the garden. Hot or chile pepper varieties offer slender, 1- to 6-inch-long, conical fruit in a festival of colors like red, yellow, orange, purple, and green (sometimes all on one plant). Sweet or bell pepper selections produce plump, roundish fruit that grow to roughly 4 inches long and 3 inches wide and offer similar brilliant colors. Breeding efforts have also concentrated on making the average (up to 5-inch-long) ovate leaves a bit more interesting. Cultivars like 'Jigsaw' produce variegated leaves with purple and white markings, while 'Black Pearl' flaunts solid deep purple foliage. Pepper plants range in size from 4 to 36 inches tall and 12 to 24 inches wide, depending on the cultivar. As with most plants, occasional insects and diseases are possible, though deer rarely pay peppers a visit. These tender perennials are warm-season plants that are treated like annuals. Do not set them out until after the threat of frost has passed and temperatures are consistently above 60°F. For a bushier, more fruitful habit, pinch the tips back to the first set of leaves in early summer. Some gardeners also like to grow chile peppers indoors as houseplants. Do not even think about saving the seed from hot peppers without using gloves. They will burn your fingers just as they burn your taste buds.

Cynara cardunculus (center) surrounded by a *Catharanthus roseus* cultivar. Taken at Linden Hill Gardens.

Cardoon

Cynara cardunculus and cultivars, zones 7 to 10
Spring to fall (foliage), summer (flowers)

Full sun; moist, well-drained, fertile soil

Cardoon is a close relative of the globe artichoke (*Cynara scolymus* and cultivars, zone 8) with an impressive architectural form. Most people who have never seen this plant (and even those who have) make a beeline for it in the garden. Huge, silvery, spiny leaves and stems make up this perennial's 4- to 6-foot-tall and 3-foot-wide stature. In summer it produces smaller, purple, artichoke-like flowers that are up to 3 inches across (too small to eat). The plant stalks can be blanched and eaten, but most people find the process of preparing the stems (wrapping with paper or other light-blocking material in autumn to tenderize) too cumbersome. Whether or not you grow it as a food crop, cardoon is a priceless specimen in the mixed border, creating edgy texture that just about any plant can be paired with. Few pests and diseases trouble this plant, including deer, though aphids may show up on occasion. Cultivars such as 'Porto Spineless' feature variable flower colors and spineless leaves, if you are interested in seeking them out. The straight species is pretty magnificent, however.

Lactuca sativa 'Royal Oakleaf'.

Lettuce
Lactuca sativa cultivars, annual
Spring and fall (foliage)

Full sun; moist, well-drained, fertile soil

While a head of iceberg lettuce sitting in the grocery store may not seem all that exciting, there are oodles of leafy options that are downright gorgeous in mixed plantings. Lettuce leaves come in all shapes (from deeply cut edges to rounded lobes), colors (shades of green and red), and sizes. These cool-season annuals typically grow 6 to 12 inches tall and wide, either as a head lettuce or looseleaf clumper. The clumpers like 'Red Salad Bowl' tend to be the most colorful and intriguing. They are also super easy to grow from seed. Just before an early-spring or late-summer rain, simply sprinkle the seed on the soil and lightly graze the surface with the back side of a rake. Make sure the soil stays moist and you will see lettuce sprouting in about week. If you do not feel like investing in spring or fall annuals, lettuce is an excellent, inexpensive filler. It is also handy to have around when you want to whip up a fresh salad. Cut the greens while the leaves are young (2 to 6 inches long) for the best flavor. New leaves will appear again in no time. If rabbits and deer are in the neighborhood, do not be surprised if they also partake in your bounty. The party is over once plants bolt. To enjoy lettuce in the summer months, seek out more heat-resistant cultivars like 'Jericho' and place them in a location that gets some relief from hot afternoon sun.

Parsley
Petroselinum crispum cultivars, zones 6 to 9
Spring to summer (foliage)

Full sun to partial shade; moderately moist, well-drained, fertile soil

The dinner table is not the only place where parsley makes a good garnish. In the garden it makes a wonderful low-growing edger with a pleasing lacy, ruffled, or curly texture. The bright green leaves grow to just over an inch long, while the entire plant can reach 6 to 24 inches tall and wide. There are lots of cultivars to choose from. They supply a wide range of plant sizes, leaf forms, and various shades of green. 'Moss Curled' and 'Petra' are classic curly varieties that offer lots of texture. Parsley is a cool-season biennial grown as an annual and produces small, insignificant, yellow-

1. *Petroselinum crispum* 'Moss Curled'.

2. *Phaseolus coccineus*. Taken at The New York Botanical Garden.

green flowers. It is an excellent bedding and container companion; its frilly foliage makes other flowering plants "pop." Parsley is seldom bothered by deer but is susceptible to rot, leaf spot, and a few insects. Do not be too quick to eradicate all the little buggers, however. Black swallowtail larvae (also known as parsleyworms) like to feed on plants before transforming into beautiful butterflies.

Runner bean
Phaseolus coccineus and cultivars, zones 10 to 11
Summer (flowers)

Full sun; moist, well-drained, average to fertile soil

For gardeners looking for an edible climber, runner bean is an excellent choice.

The straight species, scarlet runner bean (*Phaseolus coccineus*), is a commonly found option that serves up handsome clusters of red, 1-inch-long-and-wide blossoms. The flowers are a favorite among hummingbirds. Equally attractive cultivars bloom in shades of orange, pink, or white, and some are bicolored, like salmon-red and white 'Painted Lady'. 'Sunset' is a lovely pale pink option. The nearly heart-shaped leaves are not too shabby either as they expand to 5 inches long. Runner beans are fast-growing vines that can reach well beyond 8 feet long, so give them a fairly sturdy structure to climb. Dwarf varieties may be found out and about. Although perennial in places like Mexico, they are grown as annuals. Plants are easy to start from seed—just directly sow seed in the garden after the threat of frost has passed and days are consistently warm. Once they take off, you can expect 6- to 10-inch-long beans to follow the flowers. If you plan to eat the pods, it is best to harvest them at about half that size. You can also harvest them at maturity and use them as shell beans. Pests and diseases are rarely a problem, except for deer. Runner beans perform better in areas with cooler summer nights, especially while flowering and fruiting.

Nasturtium

Tropaeolum majus and cultivars, zone 11
Summer (flowers)

Full sun; moist, well-drained, average to lean soil

The peppery leaves of nasturtium are a welcome addition to salads and the mixed border. At roughly 2 inches wide, the wavy, rounded leaves add a soft appearance to any setting as the plant stems creep and sometimes climb in the garden. Mounding nasturtiums can grow 6 to 12 inches tall and 36 inches wide. Climbers can reach up to 8 feet or more in length and can be guided to scale trellises, fences, or any other nearby structure. Variegated cultivars like 'Alaska' offer a nice green and white marbled effect. The edible flowers, which are also good in salads, shine throughout summer in bright shades of red, orange, and yellow. The Whirlybird series is a standard among nasturtiums, offering the full spectrum of vibrant flowers. 'Milkmaid' is

a yellow-flowering cultivar. 'Peach Melba' produces beautiful, pale apricot blooms—by late spring most seed sellers are sold out of it. Nasturtiums can experience occasional, minor insect damage but are rarely ravaged by deer or diseases. While nasturtiums do not like excessively hot summer temperatures, a location with some afternoon shade can help get them through the warmest months. Otherwise, these tropical perennials are easygoing plants that can be effortlessly started by directly sowing seed in the garden when the threat of frost has past.

8 Vines

Although vines fill a small niche in the nonstop garden, they are fun and handy plants to have around. Winding through garden structures like trellises, tuteurs, or fences, climbers are the perfect choice for softening and accenting the hard edges of fixed materials.

Clematis 'Jackmanii Superba' (left) and *Rosa* 'New Dawn' (top and right) are like peas in a pod when it comes to sharing a sturdy structure. Courtesy of *Fine Gardening*, taken at a Jerry Fritz Garden Design project.

Flowers are a highly coveted feature for vines, as they are for most garden plants. Climbers bloom anywhere from late spring to early autumn and in a wide range of colors. Most are fairly vigorous growers, so they are not for the faint of heart. Give them their preferred conditions, adequate support, and some guidance, however, and they will enliven the otherwise drab nooks and crannies that most plants cannot reach.

Fiveleaf akebia

Akebia quinata and cultivars, zones 4 to 8
Spring to fall (foliage), spring (flowers)

Full sun to partial shade; moderately moist, well-drained, average soil

One look at the oblong leaflets on this vine and you will know why it is nicknamed fiveleaf akebia. The blue-green leaflets are held in attractive clusters throughout the gardening season, sometimes year-round in warmer climates. In spring, cupped, chocolate-purple flowers, which grow to about an inch across, dangle among the leaves—the obvious reason for the alternate moniker of this species, chocolate vine. The blooms are superseded by unique purple seedpods. White- and pink-flowering varieties like 'Alba' and 'Rosea' are also available. For a complete change of pace, 'Variegata' offers white-splashed foliage and pale pink flowers. A rare, unconfirmed cultivar called 'Kohin Nishiki' is also floating around; it is said to have white and pink mottling on the leaves and dark wine-purple blooms. It is not uncommon for akebias to reach 30 feet in length. As with many vines, their enthusiastic growth will need some prun-

ing to keep them in check. It is best to cut stems back to fit their structure and remove rangy growth just after the flowers fade. Akebias can take some drought, are deer resistant, and are great for large, sturdy structures like brick walls and pergolas.

Cross vine

Bignonia capreolata and cultivars, zones 6 to 9
Spring (flowers), summer (seedpods), fall (foliage)

Full sun to partial shade; moist, well-drained, fertile soil

This underused North American native is a fast grower, able to scramble up a sturdy fence or barn in no time. In late spring it displays 2-inch-long, flared trumpet flowers that vary in shades of red with a wash of yellow on the inside.

The blooms are a hit with gardeners and hummingbirds alike. 'Tangerine Beauty' has breathtaking scarlet blooms with an orange interior, while 'Atrosanguinea' sends out a profusion of brick-red blossoms. Cross vine has no beef with any serious diseases or pests, except for deer. It can reach well over 30 feet long in the wild as it makes itself at home up tree trunks. Plants do not get as large in cultivation but do require pruning to keep them within bounds. Because the flowers appear on the previous year's growth, it is best to cut stems back just after flowering. When cross vine is not in bloom, its 4- to 7-inch-long, lance-shaped leaves hold down the fort. In autumn the dark green leaves can take on a handsome color in cooler areas, looking as though they were dipped in a glass of merlot. Keep an eye out for cross vine's interesting, 6-inch-long, brown seedpods as well. Some gardeners in zone 5 have had no trouble growing this vine.

Trumpet vine

Campsis radicans and cultivars, zones 4 to 9
Summer (flowers), summer to fall (seedpods)

Full sun; any moderately moist to dry, well-drained soil

Hummingbirds are also attracted to this vine when it blooms in summer. Native to the southeastern United States, trumpet vine draws lots of attention with its ruby-orange, 2- to 3-inch-long trumpet flowers. Cultivars show slight variations on this color. Yellow trumpet vine (*Campsis radicans* f. *flava*) does expand the palette to an orangey yellow. Through the remainder of the gardening season,

Bignonia capreolata 'Tangerine Beauty'. Courtesy of Monrovia.

Although flowers are nice, sometimes bigger issues need to be addressed than how to make an area look pretty. When you need to hide an eyesore like a yard utility area or want to create some privacy between you and your neighbor, foliage vines are just the ticket. Their flowers may be insignificant, but their leaves create lush backdrops and screens for at least three seasons. The next time you have an unsightly fence to hide or a view to conceal, consider enlisting the help of one of these leafy climbers. Virginia creeper and wood vamp are great North American natives for warmer climates, while hops, kiwi vines, and native Dutchman's pipe are good choices for gardeners farther north. Boston ivy and grapes are good all-around options, except for gardeners in states along the West Coast, where they are known to be aggressive. Always check your regional invasive plant listings.

1. *Humulus lupulus* 'Aureus'.
2. *Parthenocissus quinquefolia* (syn. *Vitis quinquefolia*).

***Actinidia* species and cultivars** (kiwi vine, zones 3 to 9, full sun)

Aristolochia macrophylla (syn. *A. durior*, Dutchman's pipe, zones 4 to 8, full sun to partial shade)

***Cissus discolor* and cultivars** (rex-begonia vine, zone 11, partial to full shade)

***Decumaria barbara* and cultivars** (wood vamp, zones 6 to 9, partial shade)

***Humulus lupulus* and cultivars** (hops, zones 4 to 8, full sun to partial shade)

***Kadsura japonica* and cultivars** (Japanese kadsura, zones 7 to 9, full sun to partial shade)

***Parthenocissus quinquefolia* and cultivars** (syn. *Vitis quinquefolia*, Virginia creeper, zones 4 to 9, full sun to shade)

***Parthenocissus tricuspidata* and cultivars** (syn. *Vitis inconstans*, Boston ivy, zones 4 to 8, full sun to shade)

***Schizophragma* species and cultivars** (Japanese hydrangea vine, zones 5 to 9, partial shade)

***Vitis* species and cultivars** (grape, zones 5 to 10, full sun to partial shade)

Although tender climbers are not hardy and are typically grown as annuals, they are well worth planting every year for the floral extravaganza they produce throughout the summer. All they ask is for a sunny spot, adequate water and nutrients, and a support to ascend. A great many options are available, from yellow-flowering canary creeper and black-eyed Susan vine to pink-flowering bougainvilleas and mandevillas. Because they are tender, you never have to settle on just one; you can try a different selection in the same spot every year.

Bougainvillea **cultivars** (zones 9 to 11)

Cobaea scandens **and cultivars** (cup-and-saucer vine, zones 9 to 11)

Ipomoea **species and cultivars** (morning glory, annual)

Lablab purpureus **and cultivars** (hyacinth bean, zones 9 to 11)

Lathyrus odoratus **and cultivars** (sweet pea, annual)

Mandevilla **species and cultivars** (zones 10 to 11)

Passiflora **species and cultivars** (passion flower, zones 6 to 11)

Thunbergia alata **and cultivars** (black-eyed Susan vine, zones 10 to 11)

Tropaeolum peregrinum **and cultivars** (canary creeper, zones 9 to 10)

Vigna caracalla (snail vine, zones 9 to 10)

1. *Mandevilla* ×*amabilis* 'Alice du Pont'.　**2.** *Passiflora phoenicea*.　**3.** *Thunbergia alata* 'Lemon Star'.

Campsis radicans.

Clematis
Clematis species and cultivars, zones 4 to 11
Spring to fall (flowers)

Morning sun and some afternoon shade;
moderately moist, well-drained, fertile soil

Clematis is king of the climbers. With a few hundred species and several thousand cultivars, this genus has no shortage of variety. The impressive assortment of vines produces cup- or saucer-shaped and single or double flowers that are anywhere from the size of a poker chip to a dessert plate. The blooms come in magnificent shades of white, yellow, pink, violet, and purple, and there are even bicolored options. Depending on the variety, the flowers open anytime from early spring to late autumn.

   Clematis vines are categorized into three broad groups known as A (early flowering), B (large flowering), and C (late flowering)—also called groups 1, 2, and 3. Many subgroups exist, but unless you are an avid collector all you need to know is whether your clematis belongs to group A, B, or C. These groupings help to determine when you should prune your vine. If you cut the stems at the wrong time, you may miss out on the glorious flower display. Classic pink *Clematis* 'Duchess of Albany' (syn. *C. texensis* 'Duchess of Albany', zones 4 to 8), velvet red-purple *C.* 'Warszawska Nike' (syn. 'Warsaw Nike', zones 4 to 9), and fuchsia *C.* 'Ville de Lyon' (zones 4 to 9) are all great choices that reside in group C. Group B offers beautiful options like *C.* 'Nelly Moser' (zones 4 to 9), whose large pink petals are marked with a darker band of color down the center, or *C.* 'Sil-

trumpet vines display medium green, toothed leaves. The flowers are followed by intriguing, beanlike seedpods. These deciduous climbers can grow in excess of 30 feet long. In the wild they beautifully wind their way up tree trunks. In the garden they are well suited for solid arbors or trellises that offer ample space.

   Trumpet vines can benefit from a pruning in early spring. Cut lateral stems back to two to three buds from the main stems. Overgrown plants can be cut back hard to 12 to 18 inches from the ground. Just expect to miss a season of flowering. If left to their own devices, these vines will naturalize in an area, spreading by seed and suckers. Trumpet vines are not bothered by deer and will tolerate some shade, but at the price of flowers. For the best display, keep these climbers basking in the sun.

ver Moon' (zones 4 to 9) with charming pale lavender blooms. Early-flowering selections of *C. alpina* (zones 4 to 9) and *C. montana* (zones 6 to 9) are in group A. The gold-leaved *C. alpina* 'Stolwijk Gold' provides a wonderful foliar backdrop for its blue blooms.

Most clematis vines only need to be pruned to keep plants productive and for minor housekeeping (removing dead or damaged stems and keeping stems in bounds). Group A plants flower on old (or the previous year's) growth, so they should be pruned just after flowering. Group B vines flower on new shoots and old stems, so they should be judiciously pruned to strong, healthy buds before leafing out in early spring. Group C plants are the easiest to prune. They flower on all new growth and in spring can be whacked back hard to several healthy buds near the base.

Unlike some vines, clematis are a fairly polite clan that are not out to take over the world. Oriental virginsbower (*Clematis orientalis*) and old man's beard (*C. vitalba*) are troublemakers in parts of the western United States, while sweet autumn clematis (*C. terniflora*) has been known to be too aggressive in parts of the mid-Atlantic region, Southeast, and Midwest. Check the invasive plant listings for your area. Beyond that, most varieties are well suited for any type of climbing support you want to give them.

Hydrangea anomala subsp. *petiolaris* (syn. *H. petiolaris*). Taken at the Ginsburg Garden.

Climbing hydrangea

Hydrangea anomala subsp. *petiolaris* (syn. *H. petiolaris*), zones 4 to 8
Summer to fall (flowers), spring to fall (foliage), fall and winter (bark, stems)

Full sun to shade; moist, well-drained, fertile soil

If you love hydrangea shrubs, you will love this vine. Climbing hydrangea hits the ground running at the beginning of the gardening season with deep green, quilted, heart-shaped leaves that are large enough to cover the palm of your hand. In early summer the lush foliage is veiled with lacy, white blooms. Each flower can reach up to 10 inches wide. Deer may nibble on this climber, especially on the flowers. If plants go unnoticed, however, they make attractive foils through summer, until the leaves drop in fall and reveal the beautiful, peeling, cinnamon brown stems. Eye-catching variegated varieties such as 'Firefly' and 'Kuga Variegated' are also available, and the selection 'Skylands Giant' features larger flowers.

Climbing hydrangea prefers more shade than sun in warmer regions. When placed in the right spot it will happily wind its way up tree trunks or cloak stone walls. It requires virtually no pruning except to keep wandering stems in bounds. Any pruning that needs to be addressed should be done after flowering. Be patient with this plant at first; it can take up to three years to really get going. Once it does, however, it can grow up to 50 feet long. Give it a strong support and you will be handsomely rewarded throughout the year. This species is sometimes confused with Japanese hydrangea vine (*Schizophragma hydrangeoides* and cultivars, zones 5 to 8), which is also sometimes commonly called climbing hydrangea.

Trumpet honeysuckle

Lonicera sempervirens and cultivars, zones 4 to 9
Spring to fall (flowers), fall (fruit)

Full sun to partial shade; moist, well-drained, fertile soil

Lonicera is a large genus made up of lots of gorgeous shrubs and vines. However, because several species, like Japanese honeysuckle (*L. japonica*, zones 4 to 10), have found their way onto North American invasive plant lists, it is best to stick with native selections. Trumpet honeysuckle (*L. sempervirens*) is definitely among the cream of the crop when it comes to climbers. This deer-resistant, 10- to 15-foot-long vine sprouts red-tinted leaves in spring, which age to a lovely blue-green and are evergreen in the southern United States. Its cheery, tubular flowers debut in late spring or early summer and continue sporadically until autumn, when bright yellow to red berries appear. The impressive blooms are roughly 2 inches long, a knockout coral-red on the outside, and yellow on the inside. They are a hit with hummingbirds but only put on a good, extended show when plants are exposed to lots of sunlight. If coral is not your cup of tea, try one of the many *L. sempervirens* cultivars that offer stunning, completely yellow blooms, such as *L. sempervirens* f. *sulphurea* 'John Clayton', or variations of red with classic yellow interiors, such as *L. sempervirens* 'Magnifica'. *Lonicera sempervirens* 'Major Wheeler' is an excellent introduction that produces a profusion of red flowers. Whichever color your choose, give trumpet honeysuckle a sturdy trellis, fence, or pillar to climb, then sit back and enjoy the show. This vine only needs min-

Lonicera sempervirens 'Major Wheeler'. Courtesy of North Creek Nurseries.

imal pruning for shaping lateral stems back to their framework, which should be done right after flowering.

Cool as a Cucumber

Soft, cool colors provide a soothing effect
in the garden. They are great for areas
where you would like to relax or invite visitors
to explore. Creating a cool garden in a narrow, mostly
sunny side yard is a great way to put an otherwise rarely
visited area to good use. Lots of shrubs, bulbs, perennials,
and vines fit in well with this color scheme. Including a seating
area gives passersby a place to soak it all in, turning a regular
throughway area into a cottage garden destination.

Planting Plan

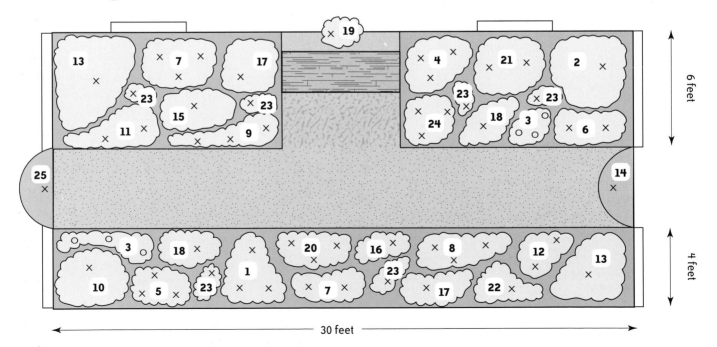

Plant List

1. *Abelia* ×*grandiflora* Silver Anniversary
   (syn. *A.* ×*grandiflora* 'Panache', zones 6 to 9) .... 3 plants

2. *Abelia mosanensis* (fragrant abelia, zones 5 to 9) .... 1 plant

3. *Allium thunbergii* 'Ozawa'
   (Japanese onion, zones 4 to 9) .... 6 plants

4. *Anemone* ×*hybrida* 'Honorine Jobert'
   (Japanese anemone, zones 4 to 7) .... 3 plants

5. *Anemone* ×*hybrida* 'September Charm'
   (Japanese anemone, zones 4 to 7) .... 3 plants

6. *Astilbe* White Gloria (syn. *A.* 'Weisse Gloria',
   zones 4 to 8) .... 2 plants

7. *Digitalis purpurea* 'Sutton's Apricot'
   (foxglove, zones 4 to 8) .... 5 plants

8. *Geranium* 'Brookside' (zones 5 to 8) .... 3 plants

9. *Geranium* Rozanne (syn. *G.* 'Gerwat', zones 5 to 8) ...... 3 plants

10. *Hibiscus* Blue Chiffon (syn. *H.* 'Notwoodthree',
    rose of Sharon, zones 5 to 8) .... 1 plant

11. *Hosta* 'Eskimo Pie' (zones 3 to 9) .... 2 plants

12. *Hosta* 'Patriot' (zones 3 to 9) .... 2 plants

13. *Hydrangea paniculata* 'Limelight' (zones 3 to 8) ...... 2 plants

14. *Ipomoea tricolor* 'Heavenly Blue'
    (morning glory, annual) .... 1 plant

15. *Iris sibirica* 'Blue Butterfly' (Siberian iris, zones 3 to 9) . 1 plant

16. *Iris sibirica* 'Blue Moon' (Siberian iris, zones 3 to 9) ..... 1 plant

17. *Leucanthemum* ×*superbum* 'Becky'
    (Shasta daisy, zones 4 to 8) .... 2 plants

18. *Pennisetum alopecuroides* 'Hameln'
    (fountain grass, zones 5 to 9) .... 2 plants

19. *Rosa* 'New Dawn' (rose, zones 5 to 9) .... 1 plant

20. *Salvia nemorosa* 'Caradonna' (sage, zones 4 to 8) .... 3 plants

21. *Thalictrum delavayi* 'Hewitt's Double'
    (meadow rue, zones 4 to 7) .... 2 plants

22. *Thalictrum rochebruneanum* 'Lavender Mist'
    (lavender mist meadow rue, zones 4 to 7) .... 1 plant

23. *Verbena bonariensis* (tall verbena, zones 7 to 11) .... 6 plants

24. *Veronica* 'Fairytale' (speedwell, zones 4 to 8) .... 3 plants

25. *Vigna caracalla* (snail vine, zones 9 to 10) .... 1 plant

Rosa 'Ballerina'.

Climbing rose

Rosa species and cultivars, zones 4 to 10
Summer to fall (flowers, fruit)

Full sun to partial shade; moist, well-drained,
moderately fertile soil

Roses are probably the most coveted of climbers. What gardener doe not "ooh" and "aah" at the sight of a rose-covered cottage, potting shed, or picket fence? Climbing roses strike a whimsical, romantic chord in all of us. These thorny climbers win our hearts with single and double flower forms that are white, pink, yellow, orange, red, and every color in between, from early summer to autumn— sometimes with repeat performances. The flowers are often followed by an attractive display of rose hips. Some varieties climb farther than others, producing canes that average anywhere from 4 to 25 feet long. Smaller plants can be grown as petite climbers or arching shrubs.

The world of roses can make even the most experienced gardener's head spin. The American Rose Society categorizes these plants into three large groups: species roses, old garden roses, and modern roses. Within these broad divisions are more than thirty subgroups or classes, such as hybrid tea, gallica, and bourbon, which are basically determined by habit and flowers. When it comes to finding climbers, all you need to know is that they can be found in a good portion of these subgroups. One subgroup, large-flowered climbers, is even devoted to the cause. You will find that some of these roses are called climbers, while others are called ramblers. Climbers are more refined; ramblers tend to be quite vigorous, with smaller flowers.

It is no secret that roses can be a persnickety bunch, often plagued by disease and pest problems. Some marquee ailments like black spot can be kept at bay by choosing resistant, hardy varieties and providing plants with optimal conditions. Give your roses plenty of room to grow—shoehorning them into the garden will only invite disease. Deer do not normally like thorny plants, but they have been known to nibble on roses.

While this vast genus ranges in hardiness from zones 2 to 11, climbers are typically hardy in zones 4 to 10. Gardeners in the colder end of that range sometimes need to provide a deep, 12-inch layer of straw mulch at the base of their roses and wrap the canes in a burlap cocoon to get the plants through winter. Most roses prefer full sun, but every once in a while you will come across a group or variety well suited for partial shade, such as hybrid musk roses. When selecting a climber, make sure it belongs to a class that is happy in your conditions. A North American native like climbing prairie rose (*Rosa setigera*, zones 4 to 9) will be fairly adaptable. Avoid invasive species like multiflora rose (*R. multiflora*) from Japan at all costs. The pale-pink-flowering, single selection *R.* 'Ballerina' (zones 6 to 9; hybrid musk) is a popular climber, as is the double, yellow-flowering *R.* 'Golden Showers' (zones 5 to 9; large-flowered climber); single, red-flowering *R.* 'Dortmund' (zones 5 to 9; hybrid kordesii); and double, pink-flowering *R.* 'New Dawn' (zones 5 to 9; large-flowered climber)—all of which produce repeat blooms.

Unless you see dead or damaged stems, do not prune climbing roses the first couple years. After that, annual maintenance pruning should be done in late winter or early spring for plants that repeat-bloom throughout the summer. Varieties that flower only once a year do so on old growth and should be pruned right after flowering to ensure blooms for the following year. Whichever time of year you do your maintenance pruning, cut secondary stems back to the main canes to just above the third or fourth bud from the base, and remove any crossing branches. Take the opportunity to trim long canes back to within the bounds of the plant's structure, and occasionally (every two to three years) remove a few old stems to make way for young, more productive canes. Overgrown climbing roses can be cut back hard to about 18 inches tall; just be prepared to miss out on the next cycle of blooms.

American wisteria

Wisteria frutescens and cultivars, zones 5 to 9
Spring to summer (flowers)

Full sun; moist to wet, well-drained, fertile soil

Some people cringe when they hear the name *Wisteria*. Invasive Chinese wisteria (*W. sinensis*) and Japanese wisteria (*W. floribunda*) have given this genus a bad reputation in many southern and eastern locales of the United States. When these impressive-yet-out-of-control vines are in bloom, it is easy to see why our ancestors brought them here in the first place. Their gorgeous lavender or white, dangling blooms enchant even the

brownest of thumbs. Thankfully the more mild-mannered North American native *W. frutescens* provides beautiful blossoms without the aggressive vining punch. The flowers are slightly smaller, 4- to 6-inch-long racemes. They may be a bit shy the first couple of years, but once they do appear they open in late spring or early summer and the show can last up to several weeks. The leaves are an attractive medium green until they drop in autumn. The vines typically extend 20 to 30 feet long in cultivation and go unnoticed by deer. Even though American wisteria is a well-behaved native, it still needs a sturdy support. A strong tree trunk, solid pergola, or stone wall will do the trick. Lots of folks just let their vines run wild. An occasional pruning may be needed to manage the size or if flowering becomes less prolific. Leave the main trunk or framework alone, but cut back any unruly lateral shoots to 4 to 6 inches long (leaving three to five healthy buds) in summer after flowering or in late winter. 'Nivea' is a nice white-flowering option, while 'Amethyst Falls' and 'Longwood Purple' are both excellent purple-flowering varieties.

Wisteria frutescens 'Amethyst Falls'. Courtesy of Spring Meadow Nursery.

Establishing Climbers

One of the great things about vines is that they are not picky about what they grow on. This leaves a lot of room for creativity when it comes to supports. Anything is fair game, from traditional trellises, walls, railings, and fences to unique found objects and homemade sculptures. The only rule is that the structure needs to be sturdy enough for the vine.

PROVIDE GOOD PLACEMENT. Once you have chosen a structure, you need to be sure that your vine starts off with a good orientation to it. Plant the vine 12 to 18 inches from the base of the structure. Tender climbers can be on the closer side, while hardy vines should be farther away to allow space for their robust woody stems and bases to mature.

ENCOURAGE A STURDY FRAMEWORK. Plan to establish a strong framework of three to five main stems, depending on the size and shape of the structure. The framework can be arranged to cover the support vertically, horizontally, and every direction in between, whichever way works best for your situation. Some vines, like clematis, will find their way up their structure on their own, using tendrils or other self-fastening plant parts—you just may need to aim them in the right direction. Others, like roses, require more help and need to be periodically trained and tied to their structure.

FEED PLANTS REGULARLY. Most vines appreciate an annual feeding of compost and a dose of fertilizer. They like fairly consistent moisture and should be given regular supplemental water during periods of heat and drought. Putting down a 2-inch layer of mulch at the plant's base will help to maintain moisture. Any pruning that needs to be done should take place according to when the vine flowers. In general, vines that flower once, and early, bloom on

Ipomoea purpurea 'Grandpa Otts' winds up a rustic, freestanding tuteur in a mixed border. Taken at the Leva Garden.

old wood and should be cut back just after flowering. Those that flower late, or throughout the season, bloom on new growth and can be pruned in late winter or early spring.

PART FOUR

FINISHING TOUCHES

Strategically placed decorative elements and structures provide visual depth to extended views. Taken at Hollister House Garden.

9 Ornamentation

Plants do not have to be the end-all, be-all when it comes to embellishing the landscape. While they are ornamental in themselves, sometimes it is nice to add a little hardware glitz to the garden. Adornments can be as subtle or bold as your personal style.

Let your creativity run wild. Garden ornaments add a sense of whimsy and permanent flair to any scene. Taken at the Auchincloss Garden.

Many gardeners limit their ornamentation to utilitarian items like benches or tables. Others prefer something a bit more eclectic like repurposed whiskey barrels or antique chimney pots. Still others fancy serious works of art such as formal marble statues, ancient urns, or modern sculpture by a commissioned artist. It is all about personal preference. Garden ornamentation is certainly not essential, but think of accessorizing your garden as if it were a woman. She may look positively lovely without makeup, jewelry, or stylish clothing, but a little frill may just put some bounce in her step.

Garden embellishments can be a handy tool to have in your design arsenal. Large-scale items such as seating, fountains, and statuary can serve as focal points or destinations. Ornaments encourage people to move through and experience the garden space. Think of a path that ends with a grouping of ordinary shrubs. Sure, they look nice from where you are standing at the beginning of the path, but do you really want to walk all that way just to have a closer look? Put a bench, sculpture, or water feature in front of those shrubs, however, and you have yourself a reason for the journey. These items appeal to our sense of curiosity and our desire to relax and soak in the atmosphere. They also help to emphasize themes. For example, elements like a classic millstone or sundial will add character and drive period gardens home, while a decorative birdbath and ornate birdhouse will round out a wildlife garden perfectly.

Because of their enduring nature, garden ornaments provide year-round interest, even during the dog days of the

Statuary creates a destination and invites visitors in for a closer look. Taken at the Thyrum Garden.

Although seating is a functional element, it can also be ornamental. Taken at the Silk Garden.

garden when not much else is happening. Beautiful, large glazed containers can be strategically placed (filled with plants or empty) in the garden to serve as focal points to mark the ends of a path or as color accents in a mixed border. Likewise, collections of objects can be displayed outdoors just as you might do inside your home. Items like antique watering cans creatively arranged on a patio table or outdoor shelving offer up long-lasting interest. No matter what you choose for your outdoor décor, be sure it is in scale with its location. If you are unsure, test out the size before placing or purchasing an item, using a similarly proportioned cardboard box, wooden stakes, chair, ladder, or any other handy object that can stand in for your work of art. If your substitute towers over its surroundings or gets lost in its setting, consider finding an embellishment with more pleasing proportions or relocating it to a better spot.

Some garden ornaments do more than just look good: they serve a purpose. Furnishings are the ultimate utilitarian adornments. Seating and tables are key components during times of socializing, moments of respite, and when we just need a helping hand. A sturdy, antique wrought-iron bench by the front door can be a useful place to set down packages as you dig for your keys, while a rustic, over-sized, wooden chaise lounge near a water feature is an ideal spot to comfortably sit down and appreciate resident dragonflies, frogs, and butterflies. Even the smallest garden has room (and need) for furnishings. Gardens are the perfect spots to enjoy a meal or drink, curl up with a good book, or just kick back and relax. Functional ornamentation can be as formal or

unconventional as you like. Moreover, if you ever want to give these elements a facelift or shake things up a bit, you can slap on a coat of colorful paint to enhance their year-round appeal.

CREATE AMBIENCE AND EXPRESS YOUR STYLE

Ornamentation is also good at creating ambience. Soothing fountains and gentle wind chimes set the tone for a calming experience, while whimsical or whirligig art and kitschy objects evoke a cheery, lighthearted atmosphere. Found objects are one of the most popular sources for creative, mood-setting embellishments. Recycled castoffs like old wine presses, brass headboards and footboards, glass railroad insulators, and architectural

1. Fun, not-so-serious ornaments can evoke a smile from even the most serious garden visitor. Courtesy of *Fine Gardening*, taken at the Cohen Garden.

2. Hand-carved figures add unique personality to mixed plantings. Taken at the Silk Garden.

pillars have many possibilities in the garden. It just takes a little stretch of the imagination.

Probably the greatest ornamental element used to create ambience from dusk until dawn is lighting. The soft glow of diffused artificial lighting throughout the garden enhances any quiet evening or bustling dinner party on the patio. It does not have to be anything fancy. Even basic, functional lighting used to safely illuminate the way to the front door or outdoor dining area offers ambience. Just do not overdo it and arrange bright lights that resemble an airfield, telling the jets where to land. You want the lighting to reveal where your next step will be, but you also want it to blend in with and accentuate the garden. This can be accomplished by placing lights where they will backlight and highlight the silhouettes of structural plants like trees and shrubs, ornamentation, and seating. Lighting used sparingly near water features such as reflecting pools can be especially magical.

Although there are many useful reasons to include garden ornaments in your plantings, do not overlook the benefit of self-expression. Talk about an aspect of gardening where you can really run wild. A garden is a place to have fun, and outdoor art is a great way to enunciate your style. You can put your stamp on the garden with even the smallest of ornaments. Colorful gazing balls, originally known as witches' balls, have been popular embellishments for years, popping up in beds, borders, and even hanging in trees. Ornaments on stakes and meaningful signs are also excellent forms of expression. Who doesn't love a good "There's no place like gnome" placard? Okay, maybe that one is not for everybody. The point is, display what makes you happy. Be as flamboyant or as subtle as your heart desires. If pink flamingos are your thing, go for it. You may get some strange looks, but in the end, who cares? It is your garden, and beauty is in the eye of the beholder.

Garden ornamentation is usually the last thing to go into the garden. Every once in a while an entire garden room is built around a centerpiece item like a major fountain or sculpture. For most people, however, embellishments pop on their radar screen after much of the earth toiling is complete, when they are casually wandering around the garden center and stumble upon the statuary section. When you are ready to walk down that path, take a step back from your garden and observe where ornamental accessories might fit in. Consider placing interesting objects around seating areas, along paths, at the end of a journey, and near entrances and exits. Place them at good vantage points, and do not reveal them all at once. Tease and coax visitors with a trail of ornamental breadcrumbs that will invite them to wander deeper into your garden sanctuary.

1. Simple lighting and textile accessories can set a cozy mood in entertainment spaces. Taken at the Gervais and Wotzak Garden.

2. Small details in a garden do not go unnoticed and often make big impressions. Courtesy of *Fine Gardening*, taken at the Crockett Garden.

10 Containers

For many of us, container gardening is the first test of our green thumbs. We begin with an African violet (*Saintpaulia* species and cultivars) sitting on the windowsill, and before we know it, our back patio is jam-packed with terra-cotta bursting with funky tropicals, veggies, and herbs.

A mix of containers is the perfect way to soften hard surfaces and enjoy plants up close. Taken at Chanticleer Garden.

The thing that makes this form of gardening so widely appealing is that anyone can do it. All you need is a pot and a plant. It does not require a lot of space, which is why it is so popular in cities, apartments, and condos. All you need to do is find plants that will work with your light conditions. You are not at the mercy of the soil you are dealt in your backyard. You have total control over the potting soil, water, and nutrients, which allows you to give your plants exactly what they need.

It should come as no surprise that containers are indispensable in the nonstop garden. These portable planting beds allow you to put plants where they would not otherwise be able to grow. Pots add life to stark locations and are perfect for front stoops, porches, courtyards, decks, and patios. They can also be used to create screening in places like a side yard or utility area where you store trash bins. Container plants soften the harsh edges of the wood, stone, and concrete used to build functional surfaces and structures. They can also add color and interest up high when they are spilling from hanging baskets and window boxes. Containers can even open the door to unthinkable possibilities—by holding desirable but rambunctious plants like mint (*Mentha* species and cultivars, zones 3 to 11), which you might never otherwise dream of planting directly in the garden.

Containers are also useful in mixed borders. Their portability makes them easy to move around, allowing you to relocate them to places that are lacking a little punch. They can fill midseason holes left by ephemerals gone by or plants that have completely failed. Pots will

Containers allow plants to grow where they normally would not. Taken at the Silk Garden.

Pots containing exotic tropicals or even lifelike plant sculptures can be placed in beds and borders to bring interest to new heights and fill seasonal voids. Taken at the Silk Garden.

One-plant pots can be used to create a portable mixed border for stark patios or entryways. Taken at the Silk Garden.

raise plants up a foot or two (or more), which allows you to create intriguing combinations with taller neighbors that are normally out of reach. You can also raise them up farther by placing them on hidden bricks or formal pedestals. Pots tucked into the border are a great way to grow tender tropicals that you want to overwinter. Instead of digging them up, just move the container to a protected location when cold temperatures start to settle in. The diverse options that containers offer are probably their greatest asset. If you do not like how things are going, no worries—just dump everything out and start over.

SIMPLE DESIGN STRATEGIES

One of the reasons why people love container gardening so much is because it never gets boring. The combinations you can create are endless as you play with color, texture, and form of both the plants and the pots themselves. There is no absolute right or wrong way to do it, but the more a planting is dictated by personal taste, the better. These miniature gardens are far more enjoyable to grow when we allow them to be an extension of ourselves—an expression of our creativity. Some gardeners take creativity to a whole new level, choosing to plant up nontraditional items like antique milk cans, teapots, or any other object that will hold soil. No matter what your pot is, you can basically go one of two routes when it comes to planting: fill it with a single variety or with a dynamic mix of different plants.

While planting a container with just one plant may not sound all that exciting at first, it will not take long before you

Some pots are so beautiful on their own that you can forget the plants and let them fly solo. Decorative pots can be used as fantastic focal points throughout the garden. They also take some of the pressure off, since you don't have to worry about keeping their inhabitants alive—just place one somewhere and forget about it for a while. Empty pots can be showcased in all sorts of spots. They work well at the beginning, end, or side of a path and as a lasting ornamental feature in a bed, border, or any space that needs a little something extra. In larger spaces, decorative containers are excellent for creating visual interest and adding depth to the scene. Because they are familiar objects, they act as a subtle frame of reference that helps anchor and put the size of the entire area into perspective when viewed as a whole from a distance. All that design mumbo jumbo aside, colorful empty pots in the garden just look cool.

Some pots are not meant to be planters—they just look good empty. Taken at Chanticleer Garden.

Tips for Success with Containers

Growing plants in pots is not rocket science, but expert container gardeners have perfected a few tricks over the years. Here are a few of those helpful strategies, which many gardeners have learned the hard way. Putting these practices into play will definitely save you some trial and error early on.

PACK YOUR POTS FULL OF PLANTS. It seems like some pots never get their groove on until it is time to dump them in autumn. If you want a lush display for summer, be generous with the number of plants that you include at planting time. If it gets a little crowded, that is what pruners are for. Selectively remove stems (or whole plants—it's okay, plants like annuals are inexpensive) to encourage good air circulation and maintain lush, healthy growth.

WATER IN THE MORNING. This gives the foliage plenty of time to dry out during the day. Prolonged wet leaves at night can lead to disease problems. Always water pots thoroughly, until you see water coming from the drainage holes at the bottom. Do not overwater, however. Allow the surface of the soil to become dry to the touch between waterings. Do not be surprised if the soil dries out within twenty-four hours during the hot summer months. Check your pots regularly.

USE A WELL-DRAINING POTTING SOIL MIX. Drainage problems can mean big trouble for pots. Plants need water, but they should not be sitting in it. The mixes offered at the garden center are formulated with excellent organic and inorganic ingredients like pine bark, peat moss, coir, perlite, vermiculite, and sand, which provide a moist yet well-drained substrate. Dirt from the backyard is usually not a good idea, and by all means be sure the pots have drainage holes.

SUPPLY PLENTY OF NUTRIENTS. Because most soilless mixes contain few nutrients, it is not a bad

Generously planting containers will result in fuller displays faster. Taken at Terra Nova Nurseries.

idea to add a granular slow-release fertilizer to the mix at planting time. Mixes that container fertilizer already are okay, but you will have better control over the type and quantity of fertilizer when you add it yourself. Container plants are heavy feeders, so also give them a water-soluble feeding every two weeks when you water while they are actively growing in summer. Mix the fertilizer at half strength if you started the season with a granular dose.

DEADHEAD AT LEAST ONCE A WEEK. This regular pruning will keep plants looking good and encourage more blooms. Do not be shy about snipping back whole stems as well. Sometimes enthusiastic growers need to be kept in check to give room to more mannerly neighbors. Likewise, some plants start to get a little tired by the middle of summer. Cutting them back by as much as half will promote fresh new growth.

Mixed plantings can pack a punch and stand out well on their own. Taken at the Thyrum Garden.

appreciate the impact single specimens supply. One-plant pots create a simple, powerful presence in the garden. Single pots can also be grouped together to build a portable mixed border that can be rearranged as often as you like. As flowers come in and out of bloom and plant habits evolve and fill in, new combinations will become apparent. Simply swapping a couple of containers around will bring about a whole new look in minutes.

For those who prefer a bit more variety all in one shot, mixed container plantings are a good choice. The easiest way to put these combinations together is to start with a heavy hitter that strikes your fancy. Choose a plant that will serve as the star of your show, a crown jewel with long-lasting attractive foliage (and maybe flowers) that is displayed on a tallish, upright habit. Let this plant serve as the leader of the pack, and select companions that will offer textural contrast yet complement the star's colors. Sticking to three or four plant varieties in one pot is a good rule of thumb. If you cram much more than that in there, your composition can end up looking a little chaotic. This companion strategy is also a good way to go about grouping one-plant pots together.

PICKING THE PERFECT POT

The world of pots is almost as diverse as the plants that go in them. Containers come in a huge array of shapes, sizes, and colors. The materials range from classic baked clay (terra-cotta) to metal to cast stone. Great improvements have been made with synthetic pots constructed of plastic and fiberglass. At first glance these containers look very similar to those made from the traditional materials that we love, but they are lighter and sometimes more resistant to cold weather. The next time you find yourself picking out a pot, keep the following considerations in mind.

If you plan to cart your pot around a lot, try to find an option made of a lightweight material. Containers made of plastic, fiberglass, and thin metals like copper or galvanized steel are easier to move around. The only caveat to that is if you want to host a large, tall plant in your pot. Bigger plants should be placed in hefty pots that will anchor them down. Otherwise, you will be spending your summer standing plants back up every time a swift breeze blows.

Some pots help retain soil moisture better than others. Porous materials like clay allow soil to dry out quickly, while impermeable substances like plastic retain moisture longer. For many folks this point is moot because containers typically require more regular watering than beds and borders anyway. However, this characteristic also impacts a pot's ability to withstand winter conditions. Permeable pots tend to crack and break when left out for the winter because the water freezes in their pores. Less porous materials like cast stone and plastic will not crack in the cold, but do not be surprised if these types of pots, as well as their watertight cohorts made of metal and fiberglass, experience some surface damage or weathering when exposed to the elements. To get the longest life out of your porous and more sensitive pots, store them in a garage, basement, or shed when they are not in use and when freezing winter temperatures settle in.

If color is your main objective, glazed pots are the answer. These wonderful

This pot is styled like pottery but is made of light, portable plastic. Taken at the Lady McDonald Garden.

Metal containers stand up to the elements better than those made of clay. Taken at Chanticleer Garden.

pieces of pottery come in every shade under the sun. There are even multicolored ceramic pots that look more like artwork than a planting vessel. The wide range of colors adds another level of flair to be celebrated and played with in the garden. Most other materials, except maybe plastic, come in more earthy tones. They may not seem as exciting, but they are easy to coordinate plants with—anything goes. Glazed pots can sometimes take a bit more thought as you find plants that will complement their sometimes jewel-like hues.

Believe it or not, the size and shape of a container can make or break a design scheme. If you have an intended place or resident for your pot, be sure its proportions match its purpose. Shallow, squat pots work best for outdoor tabletops, leaving the line of vision open for guests who may be sitting across from one another. Likewise, tall, narrow containers paired with lofty, vase-shaped plants work well in spaces where you would like to make a statement but want to leave some elbow room, such as at an entryway, along a pathway, and on the outskirts of a patio. Choosing pots that are a third to half the total height of a planting is a good rule of thumb, but do not be afraid to break the rule. Sometimes diverging from the formula leads to the greatest combinations.

1. Glazed pots offer rich, vibrant color that is fun to experiment with. Taken at the Fries and Bowers Garden.

2. Shallow containers with low-growing plants are great for tabletops. Taken at the Silk Garden.

Container Plants with Style

Among the many wonderful things about gardening in containers is their seasonality, which allows you to experiment from year to year or even month to month. When a plant fails or runs its course, it's easy to quickly replace it with something else. The best container plants are those that are easy to grow and offer the longest period of interest. Because those are also the qualities to look for in nonstop garden plants, many of the plants mentioned in other chapters are good container candidates, too. Of course, any of the tender perennials that have come to be container staples over the years are outstanding choices as well. Here is a list of container favorites. No matter which plants you choose, remember that plants are less cold hardy when kept in pots outdoors year-round than when they are in the ground. Consider potted plants less hardy by at least one zone. For example, a zone 5 plant would only be hardy to zone 6 in a pot.

1. *Cestrum* 'Orange Peel'.

2. *Dahlia* 'Wildwood Marie'.

3. *Nephrolepis exaltata* 'Rita's Gold'.

4. *Plectranthus* 'Lemon Twist'.

5. *Scaevola* 'Saphira'.

***Abutilon* species and cultivars** (flowering maple, zones 8 to 11, full sun to partial shade)

***Begonia* species and cultivars** (zones 9 to 11, partial shade)

***Browallia* species and cultivars** (bush violet, zones 10 to 11, partial shade)

***Calibrachoa* cultivars** (mini petunia, zones 9 to 11, full sun)

***Cestrum* species and cultivars** (zones 8 to 11, full sun to partial shade)

***Cordyline* species and cultivars** (zones 9 to 11, full sun to partial shade)

***Dahlia* species and cultivars** (zones 7 to 10, full sun)

***Fuchsia* species and cultivars** (zones 8 to 11, partial shade)

***Gomphrena* species and cultivars** (button flower, zones 9 to 11, full sun)

***Helichrysum petiolare* and cultivars** (licorice plant, zones 10 to 11, full sun to partial shade)

***Ipomoea batatas* and cultivars** (sweet potato, zones 10 to 11, full sun)

***Nephrolepis* species and cultivars** (Boston fern, zones 9 to 11, partial shade)

***Pelargonium* species and cultivars** (geranium, zones 10 to 11, full sun)

***Pennisetum* species and cultivars** (purple fountain grass, zones 8 to 11, full sun)

***Plectranthus* species and cultivars** (zones 10 to 11, full sun to partial shade)

***Scaevola aemula* and cultivars** (fan flower, zones 10 to 11, full sun to partial shade)

***Sutera cordata* and cultivars** (bacopa, zones 9 to 11, full sun to partial shade)

***Talinum paniculatum* and cultivars** (jewels of Opar, zones 9 to 11, full sun)

***Verbena* ×*hybrida* cultivars** (zones 9 to 11, full sun)

***Zinnia* species and cultivars** (annual, full sun)

11

Structures

In broad terms, garden structures are any nonliving, fairly permanent elements that provide a horizontal and vertical framework for a garden. This can come in the form of decking and walkways as well as fencing, trellises, and seating.

Hardscaping in the garden not only gives us secure footing but also tells us which way to go and invites us to the garden entry points. Taken at the Hall-Behrens Garden.

In addition to woody plants, large, fixed structures are often considered an important part of the bones of the garden, especially in winter. They serve as a functional backdrop for plantings and offer another layer of something interesting to look at. Sometimes these features are lumped under the label "hardscaping." Whatever their designation, they are indispensable design tools with endless possibilities.

Besides their evident functions of serving as plant supports, walking surfaces, and a place to rest, structures can be used to establish boundaries, call attention to entry points, direct traffic, and create focal points throughout the landscape and within garden rooms. Fencing is a great way to delineate space, while elements like arbors and paths help to establish thresholds and lead the way. The more interesting and noticeable the materials used to create these features, the more they will capture your attention. Whether you live on a tiny urban lot or a grand estate, no garden is complete without a few key hardscape features.

VERTICAL STRUCTURES GIVE GARDENS A LIFT

Google "garden structures" and the result will be pages and pages of options. There is no shortage of vertical structures out there, which are great at taking your attention off the ground and bringing interest up to eye level and beyond. From large pergolas and gazebos to small trellises and fences, the perfect upright architectural feature for your garden awaits. They can be purchased or, if you are a do-it-yourself creative type, built. The key is to find one that goes with your

Freestanding tuteurs are a quick and easy way to install structure and can be moved when you are ready for a change. Courtesy of *Fine Gardening*, taken at Brush Hill Gardens.

garden's style and is functionally appropriate for your setting. Structures made from wrought iron with swirly Victorian embellishments often lean more toward formal or eclectic motifs, while those constructed from rough-sawn wood or large tree branches and stout stems offer a more rustic look that fits in well with casual cottage or naturalized gardens. Many structural materials look great au naturel. If you ever want to give a tired scene a new look, however, a fresh coat of paint can easily liven things up.

Four-sided garden tuteurs and obelisks are a great choice for incorporating year-round structure in a border. At the same time, a flat, panel-like trellis is well suited for a foundation planting backed by a plain wall. Arbors are excellent for entry points and along paths. Likewise, pergolas are ideal for patios or open spaces where you wish to create some cooling shade and a cozy, intimate setting. Obviously, fences are a terrific way to establish privacy as well as divide and anchor a space. Most of these structures are usually accompanied by plants. Vines are particularly good companions,

especially if your upright architectural feature is somewhat flawed and could use some camouflaging.

Some vines, such as American wisteria (*Wisteria frutescens* and cultivars) and trumpet vine (*Campsis radicans* and cultivars), are vigorous and can make mincemeat of flimsy structures over time. Plants like these should be paired with sturdy pergolas, arbors, or stone walls, and visited by your trusty pruners if they start to run rampant. Of course, more mild-mannered annual vines like morning glories (*Ipomoea* species and cultivars) or hyacinth bean (*Lablab purpureus* and cultivars) work well on just about any structure, and allow you to test colors, textures, and forms without committing to permanence. You can also choose plants like climbing roses (*Rosa* species and cultivars) for beautiful repeat blooms that perfume the air as you walk by. Grapevines (*Vitis* species and cultivars) and small-fruiting gourds (*Cucurbita* species and cultivars), which offer edible and decorative fruit, are also possibilities.

When selecting a vertical structure, take a look around your garden and determine which areas could benefit from a little lift. Depending on the size of the structure you choose, it is often easier to start with the structure and then introduce plantings. It may be worth it, however, if a certain amount of finagling is needed to get a vital fixture into an established garden. Upright structures add depth and dimension to the nonstop garden. The verticality creates interest in a flat space, eliminating the "pancake effect" that occurs when most everything sits on the same plane. You can create long spans of seasonality by combining

1. This structure is serving double duty as a plant support and garden room boundary. Courtesy of *Fine Gardening*, taken at the Albert Garden.

2. Vines like ornamental grapes (*Vitis* species and cultivars) pair well with sturdy structures, offering attractive foliage and fruit. Courtesy of *Fine Gardening*, taken at Ferguson's Fragrant Nursery.

3. Custom fencing, such as this Japanese-style fence, is a great way to enhance a space and make it feel more intimate. Courtesy of *Fine Gardening*, taken at the Leonard and DiGiovanni Garden.

Brick is a great, sturdy choice for patios or walkways and creates an excellent color contrast for nearby plants. Taken at the Hardiman Garden.

structures with plants that have attractive flowers, foliage, fruit, and stems that step into the spotlight at different times throughout the year. Small trees and shrubs are good for adding interest in winter, when a structure like an arbor may look a little forlorn. If you plan on using a structure that people will walk under, be sure to provide plenty of headroom. Anything lower than 7 feet tall could lead to a bump on the head or a woody vine in the eye.

PAVING PROVIDES INTEREST UNDERFOOT

Paving is a very useful structural element that is often unjustly given minimal consideration in the garden. From simple gravel to exotic hardwood decking, paving materials provide a valuable utilitarian surface that tells us which direction to walk and stands as the foundation for garden rooms like dining areas. Beyond its functional purposes, paving serves as a perpetual design element. The colors and textures of patios, walkways, and courtyards deliver year-round appeal. You can even take it a step further by incorporating custom details like homemade stepping-stones, unique tiles, or eye-catching patterns, which heighten interest with a touch of original flair.

As with vertical structures, paving options span a full range of natural to composite materials like granite and concrete. These materials also come in lots of shapes and sizes. Explore your options and find the material that fits your style and budget. Precisely cut concrete pavers work well in formal gardens, while rough-cut fieldstone or gravel is great for informal settings. Wood and plastic deck-

Wood is not just for decks but can also be used for elevated paths, especially through damp areas. Courtesy of *Fine Gardening*.

Tips for Success with Structures

Because structures come in assorted sizes, it is not difficult to find the right one for a specific space. When making your selection, remember to keep scale in mind. Take a good look at your garden before adding a permanent structure. The proportions of something like a pergola can make a big difference, turning an attractive feature into an overwhelming behemoth. This is particularly a problem in small gardens, where overly large structures can make the space seem even smaller. In some cases, however, you may actually want the structure to dominate the scene, such as when you would like a vertical trellis to hide the ugly wall of a storage shed. Here are a few strategies that can help you get it right.

TAKE A TEST RUN. One way to explore which structural dimensions might be appropriate for your space is to set up substitute objects of various sizes, like a stepladder or bamboo stakes for vertical structures and garden hoses to outline potential paving areas. Then step back and see how it looks. This approach is good for smaller structures. For larger structures, test them out on paper. Take a digital photo of your garden from several vantage points and print several copies of the images on regular office paper. Then put pencil to paper and sketch various simple structures until you find an option that fits the scene. This technique is also useful when you are trying to select plants to include in your landscape.

PLAY WITH PERSPECTIVE. As you are mapping out your structural plan, do not forget to take advantage of design tricks of the trade. Just as an oversized structure can make an area seem smaller, strategically placed features that are in scale with the surroundings can make a space appear more expansive. Placing structural focal points the farthest visual distance possible will enlarge an area, as will repeating a few similar structures throughout the space. This is particularly true for narrow side yards or city lots, which can be perceived as larger just by creating a visual rhythm with a series of arbors or trellises. Likewise, using a structure like a fence or arch to frame a distant view or focal point gives the illusion of more space. This technique is rather handy if your property is surrounded by interesting vistas. Your neighbor's gorgeous weeping cherry (*Prunus* species and cultivars) may not be part of your garden, but that does not mean you cannot borrow the view.

TIE IT ALL TOGETHER. Just as with plants, structures can be linked together and with the rest of the garden by employing repetition. This can be done with color or by literally duplicating the feature. A back patio pergola can be mimicked with a smaller, appropriately sized version built off of a nearby garden shed or barn to tie the two garden areas together. Likewise, repeating the striking, glossy cobalt blue of a container on your favorite Adirondack chair will visually unite a scene. Color echoing is a fabulous design tool that can create a cohesive whole as it plays off the features of your house, such as shutters or doors, and off plant flowers, foliage, and fruit. Not everything has to match, though. Put this strategy into play with a light hand, keeping in mind that less is more.

The large pergola attached to this house is repeated in miniature on a nearby garden shed, a design trick that helps tie the garden together. The doors to both house and shed are also the same shade of blue. Taken at the Silk Garden.

Creating a focused view through a structure helps a garden seem larger. Taken at Chanticleer Garden.

Paving can also serve as a work of art, providing a unique focal point. Taken at the Hardiman Garden.

ing works well with any style and can be used for building a deck off the house or a slightly elevated path through a wet or naturalized area. Native materials found close to home or options made locally tend to be less expensive.

Do not be afraid to mix and match materials. Bringing together two types of paving, such as bluestone and brick, can help make a surface more interesting, visually break up expansive areas, and indicate when there is an elevation or spatial change. To keep your patio or walkway from looking chaotic, however, limit yourself to one dominant material and one, maybe two, accent materials. Multiple materials can also be used to differentiate main thoroughfares from secondary passageways. Using something like sandstone slabs for the direct path from the driveway to the house and gravel for the meandering paths through the garden is a subtle way to tell visitors which path is the main drag and which is for exploring. This tactic makes it simpler both visually and physically to find your way.

Before making your final paving decision, do not forget to consider durability and maintenance. A stone like slate that easily chips and breaks from freezing and thawing moisture is probably not a good idea for someone in the far north, while natural decking may not be ideal for someone looking for a maintenance-free material. If you live in an area that receives lots of rain, avoid a surface that is slippery when wet. Once you have made your selection, try to put your paving in place before installing plants and at the same time you install large, vertical structures. It is much easier to install

Although not so obvious as other elements, dining furniture also provides structure and helps to define a space. Taken at the Gardens at Northview.

Outdoor furniture can easily be given a boost with a fresh coat of paint and a little creativity. Taken at Chanticleer Garden.

these surfaces if you do not have to work around a lot of existing plants or features. Remember, main paths should be wide enough to accommodate two people walking side by side (at least 5 feet wide), while side paths can be narrower but should not feel cramped (no less than 2 feet wide).

FURNISHINGS OFFER A FINISHING TOUCH

While outdoor furniture may not be the first thing to come to mind when you think of garden structure, it is the cherry on top and probably the easiest form of hardscaping to include in any setting. A dining table and chairs require little more than a flat surface and can be readily placed on a patio, deck, or terrace to instantly create an outdoor entertaining area, while benches, chaise lounges, and side tables can be positioned throughout the garden to sanction relaxing nooks and crannies. Furniture can also be easily moved around.

As with most things, picking outdoor furniture depends on your particular style and bank account. Old and interesting pieces can be found out and about, as can refurbished items, although these can be more expensive if labeled antique or vintage. Furniture made from weather-tough hardwood, such as sustainably forested teak, is especially popular and develops an attractive shade of gray as it ages outdoors. Materials such as wrought iron, aluminum, and woven fibers are also available. Benches and other seats are usually more comfortable to sit on when backed by a wall or tall plants rather than out in the open. On the other hand, patio furniture is easier to use when given a wide berth. Give people plenty of room to navigate around a dining area; leave at least an open 3-foot perimeter around your outdoor dining table.

Most furniture can be painted, which gives you lots of room to experiment with all sorts of colors. This is where many gardeners let their wild and wacky side come out, adding a splash of bright lime green, hot pink, sunny yellow, cobalt blue, or a fun, funky pattern. When you are ready for a change, all you need to do is buy more paint. Of course, the natural tones of materials like wood offer a neutral palette that blends well with any surrounding color scheme. This is a good choice if you change up the colors of your plants or outdoor accessories regularly. Using a wood sealer on these pieces will extend their life. Furniture made of wrought iron lasts forever but does suffer from chipping paint from time to time. Because many of us are enamored of changing colors, however, this may be considered a good thing.

If you are looking for a little relaxation and whimsy, garden swings and hammocks may be the furnishings for you. Lounging about in these stress-busters is sure to melt your worries away at the end of the day, and people of all ages can enjoy them.

Many gardeners find themselves too distracted by the weeds or plants they see that need attention, or by nosy neighbors, to take advantage of the seating in their own gardens. You can block out any backyard worries with a decorative outdoor curtain or panel. These quick, stylish screens are perfect when you want to arrange a tête-à-tête, feast, or other activity that you do not want your neighbors to gossip about. Accessories and structures like these also allow you to put your own personal stamp on your garden. And as we all know, individualism is a highly cherished attribute among gardeners.

12 Seasonal Beauty and Interest

Because plants solely operate on Mother Nature's timetable, ever-changing seasonal beauty plays a large role in the garden. For many gardeners, summer hosts the ultimate smorgasbord of botanical "oohs" and "aahs," while winter serves up more subtle, single servings.

In this midsummer scene, pockets of gold brighten a shady bed containing *Dicentra spectabilis* 'Gold Heart' (top center), *Kirengeshoma palmata* (top right), an *Astilbe* cultivar (left of center), *Hosta* 'Saint Paul' (right of center), an *Impatiens* cultivar (bottom left), *Astrantia* 'Moulin Rouge' (bottom center), *Geranium* 'Jolly Bee' (bottom center), and *Carex morrowii* 'Ice Dance' (bottom right). Taken at the Benner Garden.

No doubt about it, flowers have historically been the most widely coveted plant characteristic, and rightfully so, as they provide a phenomenal display of unique color. Just do not overlook the beauty that also lies within fruit, leaves, stems, bark, and form. The interplay of all these qualities heightens the level of appeal and interest from season to season, resulting in an engaging nonstop garden. Please also see "Peak Performance at a Glance" at the end of the book.

THE PROMISE OF SPRING

We all know that spring is a time for new life, rejuvenation, and all that other stuff. For many of us, the main thing we are concerned about is being able to enjoy being outside again. There is nothing like working in the garden on a warm spring day to chase away winter cabin fever. Your muscles might be sore for a day or two afterward, but it is worth it. Spring in the garden is like a shiny new car—everything looks unblemished and filled with promise. Once you get those first couple scratches and dents, you just roll with it as the not-so-perfect reality of gardening settles in. When planning your nonstop garden, be sure to include some spring jewels that will get you in the gardening spirit and squash those winter doldrums.

Work with your setting, not against it. Face it, not every plant we see in magazines, catalogs, and books is the right fit for our gardens. We may love them on the page, but some exotic plants can quickly turn into the banes of our existence as we struggle to keep them

Opuntia versicolor (top left), *Berlandiera lyrata* (bottom left), *Opuntia fulgida* (center), *Verbena tenuisecta* (bottom right), and *Echinocactus grusonii* (bottom right) in Tucson, Arizona. Courtesy of *Fine Gardening*.

Taxus baccata 'Fastigiata' (top left), *Sambucus racemosa* 'Sutherland Gold' (top center), *Sambucus nigra* f. *porphyrophylla* Black Beauty (syn. *S. nigra* f. *porphyrophylla* 'Gerda', top right), *Yucca recurvifolia* (left of center), a *Lilium* cultivar (right of center), *Hakonechloa macra* 'Aureola' (bottom left), *Liriope muscari* 'Pee Dee Gold Ingot' (bottom center), and *Kirengeshoma palmata* (bottom right). Taken at Chanticleer Garden.

alive. Hydrangeas (*Hydrangea* species and cultivars, zones 3 to 9) are not meant to grow in the Arizona desert, just as most barrel cacti (*Echinocactus* species and cultivars, zones 4 to 11) are not too keen on the northern highlands of Wisconsin. For the least amount of frustration, stick with plants that are proven in your hardiness zone and annual moisture rate (see photo, page 205). Of course, do not be afraid to push the envelope sometimes. Chocolate flower (*Berlandiera lyrata*, zones 5 to 9) was once thought to only thrive in the Southwest but has proven to be hardy as far north as zone 5. Otherwise, if you must have a regionally inappropriate plant, expect that it will take more care. Lots of regional gems can be grown as annuals, under glass, or brought indoors when needed. Also consider looking for a related species that may be more heat or cold tolerant than the original plant that caught your eye. Prickly pear (*Opuntia* species and cultivars, zones 4 to 11), barrel cactus, and verbena (*Verbena* species and cultivars, zones 3 to 11) are just a few sun-loving plants that belong to genera that offer species with various hardiness ranges.

Create visual appeal with texture. While they may not seem as showy as some of the other choices on the rack, garden schemes that function like a reliable little-black dress or suit will keep things looking sharp through the growing season. Bring together a mix of plants with good-looking foliage and you will have a planting that shines with little effort, starting in spring and continuing into fall. The foliage does not have to be especially colorful. Combinations that celebrate varying shades of green are wonderfully simple and elegant. Just be sure your plant choices bring some textural and size variation to the table (see photo, opposite). Elder (*Sambucus* species and cultivars, zones 3 to 9) and yew (*Taxus* species and cultivars, zones 2 to 8) offer a nice, fine textural backdrop, while yellow waxbells (*Kirengeshoma palmata*, zones 5 to 8) and yucca (*Yucca* species and cultivars, zones 4 to 11) fill in the middle, and Japanese forest grass (*Hakonechloa macra* and cultivars, zones 5 to 9) and lilyturf (*Liriope muscari* and cultivars, zones 6 to 10) can supply cascading, grassy leaves at the edge of a bed in full sun to partial shade.

Accessorize plantings with spring blooms.

While you do not want to put all your flowers in one seasonal basket, scattering spring-blooming beauties throughout the garden is a great way to start the gardening season. Nature eases us into the awakening of the landscape with plants that bloom in pleasing, cool hues. You can also find blooms that come in richer or flashier colors. Annuals like twinspur (*Diascia* species and cultivars, zones 7 to 10) are an inexpensive way to brighten a scene. Poppies (*Papaver* species and cultivars, zones 2 to 9) are a classic, sunny choice, as are columbines (*Aquilegia* species and cultivars, zones 3 to 9) and foxgloves (*Digitalis* species and cultivars, zones 3 to 10) for partially shaded sites. Of course, herbaceous plants are not the only ones with spring flowers. Shrubs like allspice (*Calycanthus* species, cultivars, and hybrids, zones 4 to 9) and weigela (*Weigela* species and cultivars, zones 3 to 9) are great for areas that receive full sun to partial shade.

1. *Digitalis purpurea* 'Camelot Rose'.

2. ×*Sinocalycalycanthus raulstonii* 'Hartlage Wine'.

Fill in cracks and crevices. Whether they find their way on their own or with the help of a gardener, plants that grow in cracks and crevices are a charming addition to the garden. If you have self-sowers in nearby beds, they will usually find their way to openings or gravel on paths and patios. You can also drop some of your own chosen seeds in these locations. Forget-me-nots (*Myosotis* species and cultivars, zones 3 to 9) send out gorgeous blue blossoms in spring, but many other choices will produce attractive blooms at other times of the year. If you have large pockets available at the base of a retaining wall or in between patio stepping-stones, you can plant young, small starts and let them fill in. Petite hostas (*Hosta* species and cultivars, zones 3 to 9), corydalis (*Corydalis* species and cultivars, zones 4 to 8), and ferns are good choices for shade. If you have a spot that gets a lot of traffic and you would like more of a mat-forming plant, consider woolly thyme (*Thymus pseudolanuginosus* and cultivars, zones 5 to 8) for sunny locations. Bugleweed (*Ajuga reptans* and cultivars, zones 3 to 9) will form a carpet of foliage in partial to full shade. Just put it in a place where you really want it or where it is restricted by pavement; it has a vigorous demeanor and will creep into adjacent beds and lawns before you know it.

GOT TO LOVE SUMMER

Okay, maybe not everyone loves summer. The heat, humidity, and tumultuous moisture storms leave more than a few feathers ruffled. For the vast majority of us, however, summer is a favorite time

Myosotis species (bottom center) alongside a mix of *Brunnera macrophylla* cultivars, *Digitalis* species, *Hosta* cultivars, ferns, and *Stylophorum diphyllum*. Taken at Hollister House Garden.

of year. The parade of flowers just keeps coming and complements an enormous assortment of lush leaves. We may have to give our flowering plants a little more TLC this time of year, with extra nutrients and water, but the moments we spend parked on a patio or under an arbor right in the middle of all this botanical activity make all the effort worth it. Often the hardest things about gardening in summer are deciding which plants to showcase and later seeing the season come to an end.

Knit combinations together with a theme. No doubt, stepping into a garden center can be an overwhelming experience. Even if you have a plan, it is easy to be lured off course by the sea of plant benches laid out before you. One of the easiest ways to get back on track is to decide on a color theme. Because leaves last longer than flowers, choose a mix of foliage plants that match your motif. Tropicals like coleus (*Solenostemon scutellarioides* cultivars, zones 10 to 11) and caladium (*Caladium* species and cultivars, zones 10 to 11) offer a wealth of color options and keep on trucking well into autumn. A splash of matching hues in the form of flowers can serve as the icing on the cake. Long-lasting bloomers like pentas (*Pentas lanceolata* and cultivars, zones 9 to 11) come in a wide range of colors, as do dahlias (*Dahlia* species and cultivars, zones 7 to 10), which shine throughout summer and often peak in fall in northern climates. All of these players do well in a spot that receives mostly sun and regular moisture, and all are ideal for containers.

Dahlia 'Bishop of Llandaff' (top left), *Manihot esculenta* 'Variegata' (top center), *Duranta erecta* (top right), *Pentas lanceolata* Starla Red (left of center), *Euphorbia cotinifolia* (right of center), *Solenostemon scutellarioides* 'Sky Fire' (bottom center), and *Caladium* 'Florida Cardinal' (bottom left and right). Taken at the Silk Garden.

1. *Echinacea purpurea* 'Ruby Giant'. Taken at Terra Nova Nurseries.

2. *Campanula punctata* f. *rubriflora* 'Cherry Bells'.

Select a succession of perennial blooms. Because summer is a season loaded with flowers, it is fairly easy to have a nonstop flower display in your sunny beds and orders. Just be sure to pick strong performers that peak at different times throughout the summer. Perennials like classic pinks (*Dianthus* species and cultivars, zones 3 to 10) help get the party started at the beginning of the season, and campanulas (*Campanula* species and cultivars, zones 3 to 9) pick up where the pinks left off. Yarrow (*Achillea* species and cultivars, zones 3 to 9) puts on a sizzling display in midsummer and continues to sporadically bloom into fall with deadheading. Coneflowers (*Echinacea* species and cultivars, zones 3 to 9) are also in full swing by midsummer and keep on trucking right into fall. Blanket flower (*Gaillardia* species and cultivars, zones 3 to 9) has been known to keep the whole gang company from beginning to end. These are just a few of the perennial staples available. Take advantage of their reliable yearly performances. With the right mix, you can orchestrate your own seamless display of summertime blooms.

Have fun with see-through plants. Beds and borders do not always have to look like a grammar school class picture, with the tallest in the back and shortest in the front. Taller plants that have an airy habit, such as aptly named tall verbena (*Verbena bonariensis*, zones 7 to 11), can be placed closer to the front, yet still allow you to see the kids in the back. The effect can be quite dramatic and playful, especially when bold plants like cannas (*Canna* species and cultivars, zones 7 to 11) are standing at attention in the back—creating both a textural and color contrast. Other great see-through plants include Russian sage (*Perovskia atriplicifolia* and cultivars, zones 5 to 9), tall flowering tobacco (*Nicotiana* species and cultivars, zones 10 to 11), anise hyssop (*Agastache* species and cultivars, zones 3 to 11), and ornamental grasses like reed grass (*Calamagrostis* species and cultivars, zones 5 to 9). If you would still like to finish your bed off with a nice little edger, any number of annual bedding plants, such as lantana (*Lantana camara* cultivars, zones 9 to 11), will provide lots of flower color throughout the summer when paired with any of these taller cohorts in a sunny location.

Verbena bonariensis (center), *Canna* 'Pretoria' (syn. *C.* 'Bengal Tiger' and *C.* 'Striata', right of center), and *Lantana camara* Lucky Pot of Gold (syn. *L. camara* 'Balugold', bottom). Taken at The New York Botanical Garden.

1. *Itea virginica* Little Henry (syn. *I. virginica* 'Sprich'). Taken at the Cohen Garden.

2. *Hydrangea macrophylla* Vienna (Cityline series, syn. *H. macrophylla* 'Vienna Rawi').

Give it up to summer-flowering shrubs. Herbaceous plant flowers are not the only game in town. A fair share of shrubs also give a good floral show in summer. Make sure to leave some room for plants like Virginia sweetspire (*Itea virginica* and cultivars, zones 5 to 9), which produces fragrant white flowers in early summer. In midsummer, clethra (*Clethra* species and cultivars, zones 3 to 9) sends out its own sweetly scented, almost identical white flowers. Both shrubs can tolerate a fair amount of shade but will flower better in sun. For a dose of color, include a bigleaf hydrangea (*Hy-*

drangea macrophylla and cultivars, zones 4 to 9) in a partially shaded spot. These plants have pink or blue flowers throughout summer and bloom reliably in zone 6 and higher, although some cultivars are reported to bloom in zones 4 and 5. Sun-loving butterfly bush (*Buddleja* species and cultivars, zones 5 to 9) flowers on new growth in late summer, so you can definitely count on that shrub for a good display of abundant blooms primarily in shades of purple.

Choose partners that "pop." In many gardens, summer is a time filled with rich colors. To create unforgettable combinations, choose plants that contrast in color as well as texture. A splash of deep burgundy or bright yellow foliage really helps to make neighbors stand out. Likewise, the combination of small and large leaves and flowers provides extended interest with a zing. Using a dark-colored selection of plants like amaranth (*Amaranthus* species and cultivars, annual) as a backdrop will emphasize the form and color of the plants at the front. When creating eye-popping vignettes, do not forget to include plants like boxwood (*Buxus* species and cultivars, zones 5 to 9) that provide simple, soothing patches of green, which creates negative space and directs your eye to the showstoppers or bold, focal-point plants.

AUTUMN'S LAST HURRAH

Many plants, and gardeners, breathe a sigh of relief once autumn arrives. The hot, dry days of summer have passed, and pleasing cool nights and seasonal rains have settled in. It is not unusual to see tired annuals perk back up, while late-

From top to bottom: *Amaranthus* 'Hopi Red Dye', *Solanum quitoense*, *Buxus sempervirens* 'Vardar Valley', *Zinnia angustifolia* 'Classic Orange', and *Sedum rupestre* 'Angelina'. Taken at Linden Hill Gardens.

Top left to right: *Malus* species or cultivar, *Hydrangea paniculata* 'Unique', *Chamaecyparis obtusa* 'Gracilis', *Hydrangea paniculata* 'White Moth', *Nicotiana alata* × *N. mutabilis*, *Malus* species or cultivar, and *Eupatorium maculatum*. Bottom left to right: *Pennisetum alopecuroides* 'Hameln', *Heuchera villosa* 'Palace Purple', *Hydrangea macrophylla* Endless Summer (syn. *H. macrophylla* 'Bailmer'), *Heuchera villosa* 'Palace Purple', and *Pennisetum alopecuroides* 'Hameln'. Taken at the Leva Garden.

season perennials and woody plants come into their own. Autumn is a wonderfully colorful time of year. When choosing your plant palette, consider plants that flower, fruit, and offer richly colored foliage in fall. For many, autumn in the garden is the next best thing to summer when it comes to the swirl of ornamental attributes that take center stage.

Choose a diverse mix of stalwart plants for big impact. New and unusual plants have their unique appeal, but when it comes to getting the most bang for your buck, a collection of tried-and-true plants will deliver an exceptional, in-concert performance. This is embraced as a fundamental principle of the nonstop garden because it really works. As you begin building mixed beds and borders, try to visit other nearby gardens with mixed plantings throughout the year. Take note of which plants look good and when. Put a big star next to the ones that shine with every visit and for extended periods of time. Hydrangeas (*Hydrangea* species and cultivars, zones 3 to 9) produce striking blooms from summer to fall as well as attractive fall foliage. Ornamental grasses are great for long-lasting, fine texture, while foliage plants like coral bells (*Heuchera* species and cultivars, zones 3 to 9) provide reliable leaf color. Sprinkle in a few seasonal beauties like annual flowering tobacco (*Nicotiana* species and cultivars, zones 10 to 11), and you have yourself the makings of a nonstop garden for a mostly sunny site.

Save room for late-season superstars. We are naturally drawn to whatever is in flower when we visit the nursery or garden center. Because we often find ourselves purchasing plants in spring, we sometimes forget that we need some VIPs (very important plants) for fall. When it comes to flowers, Japanese anemone (*Anemone ×hybrida* cultivars, zones 4 to 7) and sedum (*Sedum* species and cultivars, zones 3 to 11) are excellent perennial choices for shade and sun, respectively, while caryopteris or bluebeard (*Caryopteris* species and cultivars, zones 5 to 9) is a great sun-loving shrubby option. Asters (*Symphyotrichum* species and cultivars, syn. *Aster*, zones 3 to 9) and hardy mums (*Dendranthema* species and cultivars, syn. *Chrysanthe-*

Clockwise from top right: *Hydrangea quercifolia* Snow Queen (syn. *H. quercifolia* 'Flemygea'), *Caryopteris divaricata* 'Snow Fairy', *Dendranthema* 'Cambodian Queen' (syn. *Chrysanthemum* 'Cambodian Queen'), a *Solenostemon scutellarioides* cultivar, *Dendranthema* 'Sheffield' (syn. *Chrysanthemum* 'Sheffield'), *Impatiens* Sonic Magic Pink, an *Angelonia* cultivar, *Geranium* Rozanne (syn. *G.* 'Gerwat'), *Hydrangea macrophylla* 'Maculata', *Symphyotrichum tartaricus* (syn. *Aster tartaricus*), and *Cornus kousa*. Taken at The New York Botanical Garden.

Cercis canadensis (top), *Itea virginica* 'Henry's Garnet' (center), a *Geranium* species (bottom left), an *Anemone* ×*hybrida* cultivar (bottom center), and an *Ajuga reptans* cultivar (bottom right). Taken at The New York Botanical Garden.

mum, zones 3 to 9) are among the kings of the autumn bloomers. If you are lucky enough to live in a southern climate, fall-blooming camellia hybrids (*Camellia* cultivars, zones 7 to 9) are absolutely stunning in the late-autumn landscape. Foliage is a top fall attribute as well. Redbuds (*Cercis* species and cultivars, zones 4 to 9) produce a lovely yellow fall color, while shrubs like Virginia sweetspire (*Itea virginica* and cultivars, zones 5 to 9) have gorgeous red leaves. Both will take some shade, but the leaf color is more intense when the plants are given more sun. Keep in mind that woody plants are not the only show in town. Some perennials celebrate the season in colorful hues, too—bluestars (*Amsonia* species and cultivars, zones 3 to 10), geraniums (*Geranium* species and cultivars, zones 3 to 9), and lots of ornamental grasses, just to name a few.

Branch out into new territory.
Fertile loam is not the only place plants like to grow. If you have a pond or water feature, do not forget to include some water plants. If you do not have a water feature, think about getting one. They serve as excellent focal points, and water plants are amazing as their leaves and flowers grow on the water's surface, their roots anchoring them in the soil at the bottom or in a sunken pot below. When paired together, aquatic gems create wonderful combinations with their varying textures and green hues (see top photo, opposite). The colors especially "pop" among the rich colors of the fall season. You do not need a large pond to grow water plants, which are just as happy in built water gardens or simple, water-tight containers in a sunny location. Water

lettuce (*Pistia stratiotes*, zones 9 to 11), water hyacinth (*Eichhornia crassipes*, zones 9 to 11), and water lily (*Nymphaea* species and cultivars, zones 3 to 11) are classic choices. You may already be familiar with some other plants that do not mind hanging out in the water, such as elephant's ear (*Colocasia* species and cultivars, zones 8 to 11), sweet flag (*Acorus calamus* and cultivars, zones 4 to 11), and various irises (*Iris* species and cultivars, zones 3 to 10). Always check the invasive status of a plant before introducing it to the landscape. Aquatic invasives are a huge concern, especially in warmer climates where many exotics are hardy.

Show a little leg. Every square inch of the garden does not need to burst with lush green growth. The bare stems of our favorite shrubs make gorgeous focal points among leafy cohorts. Multi-stemmed trees and shrubs can be pruned to emphasize their framework. Choose three to five main stems and remove any twiggy branches a third to half of the way up from the base. Plants like serviceberries (*Amelanchier* species and cultivars, zones 2 to 9) and viburnums (*Viburnum* species and cultivars, zones 2 to 9) are excellent candidates. Back them with large-leaved plants like hydrangea (*Hydrangea* species and cultivars, zones 3 to 9) to really make the stems stand out. Also, underplant your framework focal point with low-growing ground covers such as coral bells (*Heuchera* species and cultivars, zones 3 to 9) and creeping Jenny (*Lysimachia nummularia* and cultivars, zones 3 to 9) so that the beautiful stems do not get lost behind taller growth.

1. A *Nymphaea* species (top left), *Pistia stratiotes* (top right), and *Eichhornia crassipes* (bottom). Courtesy of *Fine Gardening*, taken at Cleveland Botanical Garden.

2. *Amelanchier laevis* (center), *Hydrangea quercifolia* (top), and *Lysimachia nummularia* 'Aurea' (bottom left). Courtesy of *Fine Gardening*, taken at the Ewing and Muriel Kauffman Memorial Garden.

THE WONDERS OF WINTER

Winter is the time for a much-needed rest for both plants and gardeners. Many plants drift off into a seasonal, dormant slumber, while we catch our breath and get ready for the next round of planting and weed pulling. Just because this is the quiet time of year for many landscapes in the northern hemisphere, it does not mean our gardens are down and out. Structures and ornaments can still be enjoyed, and lots of plants offer the subtle beauty of bark, form, and evergreen foliage in winter. A few even surprise us with flowers and fruit. Winter is a time to appreciate the not-so-in-your-face gifts of nature. Even the remains of the day in the form of lingering seedheads and herbaceous stems supply us with memories of seasons past and a promise of what is to come. Without winter, we would not appreciate the other seasons nearly as much.

Anchor the border with a mix of strong plant shapes. Flowering herbaceous plants may steal the spotlight during the warmer times of the year, but structural woody plants carry a garden through the cold dormant months (see top photo, opposite). Evergreen conifers like dwarf spruces (*Picea* species and cultivars, zones 2 to 9) take center stage with their wonderful, pyramidal, green forms, while the cascading habits of deciduous trees like weeping cherries (*Prunus* species and cultivars, zones 3 to 9) and Japanese maples (*Acer palmatum* and cultivars, zones 5 to 8) add a dramatic arching contrast. The mounding stems of shrubs like Japanese barberry (*Berberis thunbergii* and cultivars, zones 4 to

8) and upright remains of ornamental grasses like maiden grass (*Miscanthus sinensis* and cultivars, zones 5 to 9) offer additional winter interest. While barberries and maiden grasses can be invasive in some parts of the United States, plenty of less aggressive substitutes, such as spireas (*Spiraea* species and cultivars, zones 3 to 9) and switch grasses (*Panicum virgatum* and cultivars, zones 4 to 9), can provide the same effect in a sunny location with average soil and moisture.

Take advantage of herbaceous evergreens for extended interest. Depending on where you live, you will find long-lasting herbaceous plant options with leaves that can be enjoyed through the winter months. Gardeners who live in warmer zones than 5 and receive little snow cover are among the many who benefit from evergreen and semievergreen perennials. To create eye-catching winter vignettes, choose a mix of plants that offers a range of sizes, shapes, and leaf textures (see bottom photo, opposite). For example, the thin, swordlike leaves of hardy yucca (*Yucca filamentosa* and cultivars, zones 4 to 10) stand out against the oval, ground-hugging foliage of vigorous bugleweed (*Ajuga reptans* and cultivars, zones 3 to 9), while the delicate, lacy, green texture of wood fern (*Dryopteris* species and cultivars, zones 3 to 9) provides a softer touch when added to the scene. A trio like this not only makes the winter landscape a little less bleak but also looks good the rest of the year when given partial sun and somewhat rich, moist soil. Gardeners in dry, temperate regions have the option of enjoying hardy succulents like agaves (*Agave* species

1. From left to right: *Miscanthus sinensis* 'Gracillimus', *Picea glauca* var. *albertiana* 'Conica', *Prunus* Snow Fountains (syn. *P.* 'Snofozam'), *Berberis thunbergii* f. *atropurpurea* 'Crimson Pygmy' (syn. *B. thunbergii* f. *atropurpurea* 'Atropurpurea Nana'), and *Acer palmatum* var. *dissectum* 'Crimson Queen'. Taken at the Leva Garden.

2. *Yucca filamentosa* (top), *Dryopteris erythrosora* (bottom left), and *Ajuga reptans* 'Catlin's Giant' (bottom right). Courtesy of *Fine Gardening*, taken at The New York Botanical Garden.

1. *Hamamelis ×intermedia* 'Jelena'.

2. *Pyracantha* 'Teton'. Courtesy of *Fine Gardening*.

and cultivars, zones 5 to 11), aloes (*Aloe* species and cultivars, zones 8 to 11), and cacti (*Echinocactus* species and cultivars, zones 4 to 11) during the winter months. These plants provide wonderful geometric forms in sunny locations.

Put beautiful blossoms, buds, berries, and bark into play. Scattering plants with interesting winter attributes throughout your beds and borders will keep your garden lively during the seasonal intermission. Some plants save their best show for winter. Witch hazels (*Hamamelis* species and cultivars, zones 3 to 8) in the north and Japanese camellias (*Camellia japonica* and cultivars, zones 7 to 9) in the south burst with spectacular blossoms, sometimes lasting for weeks on end right in the middle of the coldest months of the year. The brightly colored fruit of shrubs like firethorns (*Pyracantha* species and cultivars, zones 5 to 10) and winterberry (*Ilex verticillata* and cultivars, zones 3 to 9) begin wowing audiences in autumn and keeps the display going into early winter, sometimes longer. The plump, fuzzy buds of magnolias (*Magnolia* species and cultivars, zones 3 to 9) and pussy willows (*Salix* species and cultivars, zones 4 to 8) make an appearance toward the end of the season, while the beautiful, shaggy, cinnamon to creamy white bark of birches (*Betula* species and cultivars, zones 2 to 9) impresses throughout the year. For maximum effect, place winter beauties like these where they can be viewed from a window indoors or along a path that you frequently travel. The gems mentioned here flourish in full sun to partial shade with average soil and moisture.

Leave garden cleanup for the spring. Old habits die hard, but try to hold off on reaching for your pruners and rake until spring. Leaving dried seedheads and stems in the garden through winter can add another level of interest as well as food and shelter for wildlife. Ornamental grasses such as fountain grass (*Pennisetum* species and cultivars, zones 5 to 11) look stunning in the winter landscape blanked with a fresh layer of snow or ice. Many plants produce intriguing seedheads that linger for months. Allium (*Allium* species and cultivars, zones 2 to 11) seedheads sometimes break off from their dried stems and are blown about the garden, creating serendipitous scenes with their starburst forms, while coneflowers (*Echinacea* species and cultivars, zones 3 to 9) offer up attractive, prickly spheres in beds located in full sun and average, moderately moist soil.

Rely on embellishments and structure for unique appeal. Even in winter, garden ornaments and structures shine with their own sense of flair. Unique supports, trellises, and arbors can provide dormant plantings with something interesting to look at. Empty ornate containers and architectural embellishments continue to hold their charm despite harsh weather conditions. And while pots may not be oozing with summertime blooms, you can create pleasing container combinations by filling them with evergreen boughs or other stems and seedheads still lingering in the garden. Finally, take advantage of the stunning silhouettes many trees and shrubs exhibit in the winter landscape. Whether

1. *Echinacea purpurea.*

2. *Pennisetum alopecuroides* 'Hameln'. Taken at the Leva Garden.

it be their natural form or one created by a gardener's hand, these dramatic profiles stand out against a fresh blanket of snow or when sited near a solid backdrop such as house, outbuilding, or fence. Choose plants that also have attractive flowers, fruit, or foliage, such as apples and crabapples (*Malus* species and cultivars, zones 3 to 9), since these will provide interest at other times of the year, when winter is all but a distant memory.

1. An ice-coated garden structure. Taken at the Leva Garden.

2. A wintery container with evergreen boughs. Taken at Brush Hill Gardens.

3. *Malus* Guinevere (syn. *M.* 'Guinzam'). Taken at Hollister House Garden.

Invasive Plants

By now most people have heard a word or two about invasive plants. Unwanted thugs are wreaking havoc on our native landscape and as a result disturbing our delicate ecosystems. Be sure that you are not contributing to this problem, and avoid growing invasive plants. Just because a plant is sold at a garden center does not mean it is safe and noninvasive. Check with local state agencies such as the Department of Environmental Protection, Department of Agriculture, or Cooperative Extension offices for invasive listings before introducing any new plants to your garden. Some plants may be invasive in one area and completely amiable in others. In this book we recommend plants that are widely agreeable, but some are troublemakers for gardeners in select areas. The list below contains plants found to be invasive primarily on the WeedUS database at www. invasive.org/weedus. This is by no means a comprehensive list, but one that is related to the plants mentioned throughout this book. It is a good idea to check local lists regularly as well, as invasive plant threats are constantly changing. Remember that if a species is listed, that includes the cultivars too.

Abutilon grandifolium (HI)

Acer campestre (OH)

Acer palmatum (VA)

Acer platanoides (CT, DE, IL, IN, MA, MD, ME, MI, NH, NJ, NY, OR, PA, TN, VA, VT, WI, WV)

Acer pseudoplatanus (CT, PA)

Acer tataricum subsp. *ginnala*, syn. *A. ginnala* (CT, IL, MA, MO, NY, VT, WI)

Adiantum hispidulum (HI)

Adiantum raddianum (HI)

Agave sisalana (HI)

Ajuga reptans (MD, TN, VA)

Akebia quinata (KY, MD, NJ, PA, VA)

Allium vineale (CT, MD, NC, NJ, PA, TN, VA, WV)

Alternanthera philoxeroides (AL, AZ, CA, FL, SC, TX)

Alternanthera sessilis (AL, CA, FL, MA, MN, NC, OR, SC, VT)

Amaranthus spinosus (HI, TN)

Amaranthus viridis (HI)

Artemisia absinthium (ND, OR, WA)

Artemisia stelleriana (NJ)

Artemisia vulgaris (MD, NJ, NY, PA, TN, VA)

Asclepias curassavica (HI)

Berberis thunbergii (CT, DE, IN, KY, MA, MD, ME, MO, NC, NH, NJ, NY, OH, PA, RI, TN, VA, VT, WI, WV)

Bougainvillea glabra (CA, FL)

Brassica oleracea (HI)

Buddleja davidii (CA, KY, NC, NJ, OR, PA, WA, WV)

Buddleja lindleyana (GA, FL, NC, TX)

Buddleja madagascariensis (HI)

Campanula rapunculoides (WI)

Canna indica (HI)

Carex kobomugi (MD, NJ, VA)

Carex longii (HI)

Cedrus deodara (HI)

Centaurea cyanus (MD, TN)

Cestrum diurnum (FL, HI)

Cestrum nocturnum (FL, GA, HI)

Chamaecyparis lawsoniana (HI)

Clematis orientalis (CO, NV)

Clematis terniflora (DE, IL, MD, NJ, TN, VA)

Clematis vitalba (OR, WA)

Colocasia esculenta (FL)

Cosmos bipinnatus (TN)

Cynara cardunculus (CA)

Dianthus armeria (MD)

Digitalis lanata (WI)

Digitalis purpurea (CA, OR, WA)

Eichhornia crassipes (CA, DE, FL, GA, LA, TX)

Eschscholzia californica (TN)

Euphorbia cyparissias (CT, MA, NJ, NY, RI, WI)

Euphorbia esula (CA, CO, CT, IA, ID, MI, MN, MT, NC, ND, NE, NJ, OR, SD, UT, VA, WA, WI, WY)

Euphorbia peplus (HI)

Euphorbia pulcherrima (HI)

Festuca ovina (NY)

Festuca rubra (HI, NY)

Foeniculum vulgare (CA, HI, OR, VA, WA)

Geranium columbinum (MD, TN)

Geranium homeanum (HI)

Geranium lucidum (OR)

Geranium robertianum (OR, WA)

Geranium thunbergii (CT)

Hedychium coronarium (HI)

Hedychium flavescens (HI)

Hedychium gardnerianum (HI)

Hemerocallis fulva ((DE, IL, IN, MD, MI, PA, VA, WI, WV)

Hemerocallis lilioasphodelus (TN, VA)
Hibiscus syriacus (KY, VA)
Hibiscus tiliaceus (FL)
Hibiscus trionum (OR, WA)
Ilex aquifolium (CA, MD, OR, WA)
Ilex crenata (VA)
Impatiens glandulifera (OR)
Ipomoea alba (HI)
Ipomoea aquatica (FL, TX)
Ipomoea hederacea (KY, TN, VA)
Ipomoea lacunose (MD)
Ipomoea purpurea (AZ, KY, TN, VA)
Iris pseudacorus (CT, NC, NH, OR, TN, VA, VT, WI, WA, WV)
Lactuca sativa (CA)
Lamium amplexicaule (AZ, MD, TX, TN, WV)
Lamium maculatum (MD)
Lamium purpureum (CT, MD, TN)
Lantana camara (AZ, FL, HI, SC, TX)
Lobularia maritima (CA)
Lysimachia nummularia (CT, IN, MD, MI, MO, NJ, OR, PA, VA, WI, WV)
Malus baccata (IL)
Malus floribunda (IL)
Malus prunifolia (CT)
Malus pumila (AL, IL, MD, MT, SC, VA, WV)
Malus sylvestris (OH)
Manihot esculenta (HI)
Manihot glaziovii (HI)
Mentha pulegium (CA, OR)
Mentha spicata (CA, TN)
Mentha ×villosa (HI)
Miscanthus sinensis (CT, GA, IL, IN, KY, MD, NC, NJ, PA, SC, TN, VA, WI)
Muscari botryoides (MD, TN, WV)
Muscari neglectum (TN)
Myosotis scorpioides (CT, MI, OR, WI)
Myosotis sylvatica (WI)
Nepeta cataria (MD)
Nephrolepis cordifolia (FL)
Nephrolepis falcata (HI)
Nephrolepis multiflora (FL, HI)
Nicotiana glauca (AZ, CA, FL, HI, NV, TX)
Passiflora bicornis (HI)
Passiflora edulis (HI)

Passiflora foetida (HI)
Passiflora laurifolia (HI)
Passiflora ligularis (HI)
Passiflora suberosa (HI)
Passiflora subpeltata (HI)
Passiflora tripartita var. *mollissima* (HI)
Pennisetum ciliare (AZ, TX)
Pennisetum clandestinum (HI)
Pennisetum purpureum (FL, HI)
Pennisetum setaceum (AZ, CA, HI, NV)
Petroselinum crispum (HI)
Phormium tenax (HI)
Picea abies (HI, MD, TN)
Pistia stratiotes (DE, FL, TX)
Prunus avium (DE, MA, MD, NC, NJ, NY, OR, PA, RI, TN, VA, WA)
Prunus cerasifera (OR)
Prunus cerasus (CA, KY, MD, NC, NY, OR, WA, WV)
Prunus domestica (IN, MI, OR)
Prunus laurocerasus (OR, WA)
Prunus lusitanica (OR, WA)
Prunus mahaleb (ID, IL, MO, OR, WA)
Prunus padus (AK, AL)
Prunus persica (AR, CA, FL, GA, IL, KY, LA, MS, NC, SC, TN, VA)
Prunus spinosa (OR)
Pyracantha angustifolia (CA, HI, OR)
Pyracantha coccinea (OR)
Ricinus communis (HI)
Rosa bracteata (FL, LA, MS, TX, VA)
Rosa canina (CA, IN, MD, NJ, OR, VA, WA)
Rosa ×damascena (NC)
Rosa gallica (GA, SC, VA)
Rosa majalis, syn. *R. cinnamomea* (VT, WI)
Rosa micrantha (NC, NY, SC, VA)
Rosa multiflora (AR, CA, CO, CT, DE, GA, IL, IN, KY, LA, MA, MD, ME, MI, MO, MS, NC, NH, NJ, NY, OH, OR, PA, SC, TN, VA, VT, WI, WV)
Rosa rubiginosa, syn. *R. eglanteria* (CA, IN, LA, MA, ME, NH, NY, OH, OR, PA, VA, WA, WI)
Rosa rugosa (CT, MA, NJ, NY, WA)
Rosa spinosissima (GA, IL)

Rosa wichuraiana (KY, MS, NC, SC, TN, VA)
Salix alba (MI, NY, VA)
Salix caprea (NC, RI)
Salix cinerea (MD, NC, NY)
Salix fragilis (CO, IL, MA, MI, MN, NV, NY, UT)
Salix matsudana (MI)
Salix ×pendulina (MI)
Salix pentandra (IA, MA, MD, MI, MN, WI)
Salix purpurea (CA, MA, MI, WI)
Salix ×sepulcralis (IL, NC, NY, OR, WA, WV)
Salix viminalis (MA, ME, VT, WA)
Salvia aethiopis (AZ, OR, UT, WA)
Solenostemon scutellarioides (HI)
Spiraea japonica (KY, MD, NC, NJ, PA, TN, VA)
Spiraea prunifolia (AL, TN)
Spiraea thunbergii (NC)
Taxus cuspidata (NJ, VA)
Verbena bonariensis (GA, OR)
Verbena litoralis (invasive in HI)
Viburnum dilatatum (VA)
Viburnum lantana (IL, WI)
Viburnum opulus (IL, KY, MI, MO, NH, NY, OH, VT)
Viburnum opulus var. *opulus* (IN, PA, WI)
Viburnum sieboldii (NY, PA)
Wisteria floribunda (MD, NC, NJ, SC, TN, VA)
Wisteria sinensis (FL, GA, HI, IL, KY, LA, MA, MD, NC, NJ, NY, PA, SC, TN, VA)

Conversion Tables

temperatures

$$°C = 5/9 \times (°F-32)$$

$$°F = (9/5 \times °C) + 32$$

inches	centimeters		feet	meters
½	1.25		1	0.3
1	2.5		2	0.6
2	5.0		3	0.9
3	7.5		4	1.2
4	10		5	1.5
5	12.5		6	1.8
6	15		7	2.1
7	18		8	2.4
8	20		9	2.7
9	23		10	3.0
10	25		12	3.6
12	30		15	4.5
15	38		18	5.4
18	45		20	6.0
20	50		25	7.5
24	60		30	9.0
30	75		35	10.5
32	80		40	12
36	90		45	13.5
			50	15

Hardiness Zones

Hardiness zones are a handy way for gardeners to gauge which plants are best for their location. Please note, however, that zone recommendations are just a guide and are certainly not set in stone. Plants, and gardeners, can always prove zone recommendations wrong thanks to microclimates, regional variations, and global climate changes. See the chart below to determine which zone you live in.

temperatures

$$°C = 5/9 \times (°F - 32)$$

$$°F = (9/5 \times °C) + 32$$

PLANT HARDINESS ZONES		
Average Annual Minimum Temperature		
Zone	Temperature (deg. F)	Temperature (deg. C)
1	Below –50	–45.6 and below
2a	–45 to –50	–42.8 to –45.5
2b	–40 to –45	–40.0 to –42.7
3a	–35 to –40	–37.3 to –40.0
3b	–30 to –35	–34.5 to –37.2
4a	–25 to –30	–31.7 to –34.4
4b	–20 to –25	–28.9 to –31.6
5a	–15 to –20	–26.2 to –28.8
5b	–10 to –15	–23.4 to –26.1
6a	–5 to –10	–20.6 to –23.3
6b	0 to –5	–17.8 to –20.5
7a	5 to 0	–15.0 to –17.7
7b	10 to 5	–12.3 to –15.0
8a	15 to 10	–9.5 to –12.2
8b	20 to 15	–6.7 to –9.4
9a	25 to 20	–3.9 to –6.6
9b	30 to 25	–1.2 to –3.8
10a	35 to 30	1.6 to –1.1
10b	40 to 35	4.4 to 1.7
11	40 and above	4.5 and above

To see the U.S. Department of Agriculture Hardiness Zone Map, go to the U.S. National Arboretum site at: http://www.usna.usda.gov/Hardzone/ushzmap.html.

Glossary

Acidic: Having a pH less than 7 and sometimes called "sour." You can raise the pH with lime.

Alkaline: Having a pH greater than 7 and sometimes referred to as "sweet" or "limey." You can lower the pH with sulfur, pine needles, or peat moss.

Annual: A plant that completes its life cycle in one year, meaning that it grows from seed, produces seed, and then dies off all during one growing season.

Arbor: A shaded seating area or walkway in a garden or park formed by either a manmade structure or trained trees, shrubs, or vines to create an enclosure or frame a view.

Bolt: To quickly switch from all foliage to flowers and seeds in hot weather, leaving the leaves tough and bitter as all the energy goes toward seed production.

Bulbs: Ornamental, partial-season, mostly simple-stemmed plants with underground storage structures housing their complete life cycle, including bulbs, corms, tubers, and thickened rhizomes.

Catkins: Long clusters of same-sex flowers without petals found on willows, birches, and oaks. These plants are wind-pollinated between catkins and flowers.

Compost: Decomposed organic material.

Cooperative Extension System: A nationwide, noncredit educational network in the United States. Each state and territory has an office at its land-grant university and a network of local or regional offices providing useful, practical, research-based information to agricultural producers and the general public. These offices are a resource for regionally specific gardening information, soil testing, and pest and disease identification.

Cultivar: Contraction of "cultivated variety." Cultivars have distinct, uniform, and stable attributes after propagation.

Deadhead: To remove dead flowers for a better appearance or to encourage a longer flowering season by not allowing them to set seed.

Desiccation: The drying out that occurs when a plant is exposed to more wind, sunlight, or drought than it can withstand.

Dioecious: Having male and female reproductive organs on separate individuals of the same species. Common in winterberry hollies.

Ephemeral: Short-lived. Used to describe a plant that only grows during the best time for its survival, and that then sets seed and goes dormant.

Fastigiate: Having an upright growth habit where branching extends parallel to the trunk toward the top.

Genus, genera: A group of plants bearing common characteristics, ranked in taxonomic nomenclature between the categories of family and species.

Herb: A broadly used term to describe a fleshy (not woody), seed-bearing plant that dies back at the end of the season. Such "herbaceous" plants are not to be confused with the aromatic or medicinal plants also known as herbs, which may be evergreen.

Humus: Partially decomposed organic matter in the soil that is added to improve fertility.

Hybrid: Offspring of two plants, generated by pollinating the pistil of one species with the pollen of another.

Invasive: Tending to spread. Especially used to describe vigorous, introduced (nonnative) species that thrive outside their natural habitats. Because these plants are adaptable, aggressive, and propagate readily, they generally have no natural enemies and are disruptive to native ecosystems.

Larva: The newly hatched form of an insect that feeds until undergoing metamorphosis to emerge a changed form in adulthood.

Lateral branch: Branch growing out the sides, contributing to the development of a sturdy, well-tapered trunk.

Leaflet: A part of a compound leaf that may look like an entire leaf but grows from a vein of the whole leaf, not a stem.

Lean soil: Any soil that is not rich in organic matter.

Microclimate: The temperature, wind, humidity, and other factors for a small place in contrast to the climate of the entire area.

Monoculture: The cultivation of only one type of plant. This is the opposite of biodiversity and can sometimes be responsible for the spread of plant diseases and insect pests.

Mulch: A protective cover, composed of natural or synthetic materials, placed over the soil to protect plants from the stress associated with climate.

Native: Naturally occurring (without human actions) in a specific region, state, ecosystem, or habitat.

Naturalized: Nonnative in an area but established (without human actions) as if native.

Old growth, old wood: A stem or twig that originated during the previous season's growth or at an earlier time.

Perennial: A plant that lives for more than two years. Usually refers to herbaceous plants.

Pergola: An architectural garden feature built overhead to form a walkway with pillars that support beams and a lattice.

pH: A measure of the hydrogen-ion concentration of soil, which expresses the soil's alkalinity or acidity.

Pistil: The central female reproductive organ, including the ovary, style, and stigma.

Root ball: The solid mass of roots and soil formed by a plant in a container or in the ground at nurseries where plants are tied into burlap for shipping.

Soil microbes: The beneficial microorganisms, fungi, and protozoa that decompose organic matter and are vital to maintaining healthy, productive soil.

Species: The fundamental unit in taxonomic nomenclature, representing plants that can interbreed and make fertile offspring, or plants with similar DNA or morphology.

Stamen: The male organ of a flower, usually including filament, anther, and pollen sacs.

Trellis: A ladderlike structure, usually made from interwoven pieces of wood or metal, for supporting climbing plants.

Tuteur: An upright, multisided structure to support climbing plants.

Umbel: A flower form that has equal-length stalks radiating out from one place and small flowers in a flat display at the tips, like an umbrella.

Variegated: Showing more than one color in various arrangements—dots, stripes, splashes, or edging.

Zones (hardiness zones): A system that identifies eleven separate hardiness zones based on minimum average winter temperatures; each zone is 10 degrees F warmer (or colder) in an average winter than the adjacent zone.

References and Resources

REFERENCES

Anisko, Tomasz. *When Perennials Bloom: An Almanac for Planning and Planting*. Portland, Oregon: Timber Press, 2008.

Armitage, Allan M. *Armitage's Manual of Annuals, Biennials, and Half-Hardy Perennials*. Portland, Oregon: Timber Press, 2001.

Armitage, Allan M. *Herbaceous Perennial Plants: A Treatise on Their Identification, Culture, and Garden Attributes*. Third edition. Champaign, Illinois: Stipes, 2008.

Bailey, Liberty Hyde, and Ethel Zoe Bailey. *Hortus Third: A Concise Dictionary of Plants Cultivated in the United States and Canada*. Revised and expanded by the staff of the Liberty Hyde Bailey Hortorium. New York: Macmillan, 1976.

Baldwin, Debra Lee. *Designing with Succulents*. Portland, Oregon: Timber Press, 2007.

Bartley, Jennifer. *Designing the New Kitchen Garden: An American Potager Handbook*. Portland, Oregon: Timber Press, 2006.

Brickell, Christopher, and H. Marc Cathey. *The American Horticultural Society A–Z Encyclopedia of Garden Plants*. New York: DK, 2004.

Burrell, C. Colston, and Judith Knott Tyler. *Hellebores: A Comprehensive Guide*. Portland, Oregon: Timber Press, 2006.

Cohen, Stephanie, and Nancy J. Ondra. *The Perennial Gardener's Design Primer*. North Adams, Massachusetts: Storey, 2005.

Cohen, Stephanie, Nancy J. Ondra, and Rob Cardillo. *Fallscaping: Extending Your Garden Season into Autumn*. North Adams, Massachusetts: Storey, 2007.

Cullina, William. *The New England Wild Flower Society Guide to Growing and Propagating Wildflowers of the United States and Canada*. Boston: Houghton Mifflin, 2000.

Cullina, William. *Native Trees, Shrubs, and Vines: A Guide to Using, Growing, and Propagating North American Woody Plants*. Boston: Houghton Mifflin, 2002.

Cullina, William. *Understanding Perennials: A New Look at an Old Favorite*. Boston: Houghton Mifflin Harcourt, 2009.

Darke, Rick. *The American Woodland Garden: Capturing the Spirit of the Deciduous Forest*. Portland, Oregon: Timber Press, 2002.

Darke, Rick. *The Encyclopedia of Grasses for Livable Landscapes*. Portland, Oregon: Timber Press, 2006.

Denckla, Tanya L. K. *The Gardener's A–Z Guide to Growing Organic Food*. North Adams, Massachusetts: Storey, 2004.

Dirr, Michael A. *Manual of Woody Landscape Plants: Their Identification, Ornamental Characteristics, Culture, Propagation, and Uses*. Fifth edition. Champaign, Illinois: Stipes, 1998.

Fischer, Thomas, and Richard Bloom. *Perennial Combinations: 100 Dazzling Plant Combinations for Every Season*. Portland, Oregon: Timber Press, 2009.

Glattstein, Judy. *Bulbs for Garden Habitats*. Portland, Oregon: Timber Press, 2007.

Hodgson, Larry. *Annuals for Every Purpose: Choose the Right Plants for Your Conditions, Your Garden, and Your Taste*. Emmaus, Pennsylvania: Rodale Press, 2003.

Kowalchik, Claire, and William H. Hylton. *Rodale's Illustrated Encyclopedia of Herbs*. Emmaus, Pennsylvania: Rodale Press, 1998.

Ondra, Nancy J., and Rob Cardillo. *The Perennial Care Manual: A Plant-by-Plant Guide: What to Do and When to Do It.* North Adams, Massachusetts: Storey, 2009.

Phillips, Ellen, and C. Colston Burrell. *Rodale's Illustrated Encyclopedia of Perennials.* Tenth anniversary revised and expanded edition. Emmaus, Pennsylvania: Rodale Press, 1993.

Rice, Graham, and Kurt Bluemel. *American Horticultural Society Encyclopedia of Perennials: The Definitive Illustrated Reference Guide.* New York: DK, 2006.

Rogers, Ray, and Richard W. Hartlage. *Pots in the Garden: Expert Design and Planting.* Portland, Oregon: Timber Press, 2007.

Rost, Thomas L., Michael G. Barbour, C. Ralph Stocking, and Terence M. Murphy. *Plant Biology.* Belmont, California: Wadsworth, 1998.

Speichert, Greg, and Sue Speichert. *Encyclopedia of Water Garden Plants.* Portland, Oregon: Timber Press, 2004.

Staub, Jack. *Seventy-five Exciting Vegetables for Your Garden.* Layton, Utah: Gibbs Smith, 2005.

WEB SITES

American Conifer Society
www.conifersociety.org

Cornell University
www.gardening.cornell.edu/index.html

Fine Gardening
www.finegardening.com

Herb Society of America
www.herbsociety.org

Kemper Center for Home Gardening
www.mobot.org/gardeninghelp/plantinfo.shtml

Lady Bird Johnson Wildflower Center
www.wildflower.org

Royal Horticultural Society
www.rhs.org.uk/index.asp

USDA Cooperative State Research,
Education, and Extension Service
www.csrees.usda.gov/index.html

SOURCES

Ambergate Gardens
Chaska, Minnesota
(877) 211-9769
www.ambergategardens.com

Annie's Annuals and Perennials
Richmond, California
(888) 266-4370
www.anniesannuals.com

Antique Rose Emporium
Brenham, Texas; (800) 441-0002
www.antiqueroseemporium.com

Arrowhead Alpines
Fowlerville, Michigan
(517) 223-3581
www.arrowheadalpines.com

Asiatica
Lewisberry, Pennsylvania
(717) 938-8677
www.asiaticanursery.com

Avant Gardens
Dartmouth, Massachusetts
(508) 998-8819
www.avantgardensne.com

Big Dipper Farm
Black Diamond, Washington
(360) 886-8133
www.bigdipperfarm.com

Bluestone Perennials
Madison, Ohio; (800) 852-5243
www.bluestoneperennials.com

Brent and Becky's Bulbs
Gloucester, Virginia
(877) 661-2852
www.brentandbeckysbulbs.com

Bustani Plant Farm
Stillwater, Oklahoma
(405) 372-3379
www.bustaniplantfarm.com

Carroll Gardens
Westminster, Maryland
(800) 638-6334
www.carrollgardens.com

Cistus Nursery
Sauvie Island, Oregon
(503) 621-2233
www.cistus.com

Collector's Nursery
Battle Ground, Washington
(360) 574-3832
www.collectorsnursery.com

Cottage Garden
Piasa, Illinois; (618) 729-4324
www.cottgardens.com

Digging Dog Nursery
Albion, California
(707) 937-1130
www.diggingdog.com

Fairweather Gardens
Greenwich, New Jersey
(856) 451-6261
www.fairweathergardens.com

Fedco Seeds
Waterville, Maine
(207) 873-7333
www.fedcoseeds.com

Forestfarm
Williams, Oregon
(541) 846-7269
www.forestfarm.com

Fritz Creek Gardens
Homer, Alaska; (907) 235-4969
www.alaskahardy.com

Gardens Alive
Lawrenceburg, Indiana
(513) 354-1482
www.gardensalive.com

Girard Nurseries
Geneva, Ohio; (440) 466-2881
www.girardnurseries.com

Goodwin Creek Gardens
Williams, Oregon
(800) 846-7359
www.goodwincreekgardens.com

Great Garden Plants
Holland, Michigan
(616) 399-3448
www.greatgardenplants.com

Heronswood
Warminster, Pennsylvania
(877) 674-4714
www.heronswood.com

High Country Gardens
Santa Fe, New Mexico
(800) 925-9387
www.highcountrygardens.com

Jackson and Perkins
Hodges, North Carolina
(800) 292-4769
www.jacksonandperkins.com

J. L. Hudson, Seedsman
La Honda, California
www.jlhudsonseeds.net

Johnny's Selected Seeds
Winslow, Maine; (877) 564-6697
www.johnnyseeds.com

John Scheepers
Bantam, Connecticut
(860) 567-0838
www.johnscheepers.com

Joy Creek Nursery
Scappoose, Oregon
(503) 543-7474
www.joycreek.com

Logee's Tropical Plants
Danielson, Connecticut
(888) 330-8038
www.logees.com

Klehm's Song Sparrow Farm
and Nursery
Avalon, Wisconsin
(800) 553-3715
www.songsparrow.com

Munchkin Nursery and Gardens
Depauw, Indiana; (812) 633-4858
www.munchkinnursery.com

Niche Gardens
Chapel Hill, North Carolina
(919) 967-0078
www.nichegardens.com

Peaceful Valley Farm and
Garden Supply
Grass Valley, California
(888) 784-1722
www.groworganic.com

Pine Knot Farms
Clarksville, Virginia
(434) 252-1990
www.pineknotfarms.com

Plant Delights Nursery
Raleigh, North Carolina
(919) 772-4794
www.plantdelights.com

Prairie Nursery
Westfield, Wisconsin
(800) 476-9453
www.prairienursery.com

Rainbow Iris Farms
Bedford, Iowa; (712) 523-2807
www.rainbowfarms.net

Rare Find Nursery
Jackson, New Jersey
(732) 833-0613
www.rarefindnursery.com

Sandy Mush Herb Nursery
Leicester, North Carolina
(828) 683-2014
www.sandymushherbs.com

Sunshine Farms and Gardens
Renick, West Virginia
(304) 497-2208
www.sunfarm.com

Thompson and Morgan
Jackson, New Jersey
(800) 274-7333
www.tmseeds.com

Van Bourgondien
Virginia Beach, Virginia
(800) 622-9959
www.dutchbulbs.com

Well-Sweep Herb Farm
Port Murray, New Jersey
(908) 852-5390
www.wellsweep.com

White Flower Farm
Torrington, Connecticut
(888) 466-8849
www.whiteflowerfarm.com

Yucca Do Nursery
Giddings, Texas; (979) 542-8811
www.yuccado.com

Garden Credits

Albert Garden, Tualatin, Oregon; owned and designed by Lisa Albert.

Auchincloss Garden, Washington, Connecticut; owned by George and Judy Auchincloss; designed by Judy Auchincloss, Tami Mills, and Kent Greenhouse and Gardens (www.kentgreenhouseandgardens.com).

Benner Garden, Roxbury, Connecticut; owned and designed by Jennifer and Brent Benner.

Berkshire Botanical Garden, Stockbridge, Massachusetts; designed by staff (www.berkshirebotanical.org).

Brine Garden, Pawling, New York; owned by Duncan and Julia Brine; designed by Duncan Brine (www.gardenlarge.com).

Brush Hill Gardens, Washington, Connecticut; owned and designed by Charles Raskob Robinson and Barbara Paul Robinson (www.brushhillgardens.com).

Central Park Conservatory Garden, New York, New York; designed by staff (www.centralparknyc.org).

Chadwick Arboretum and Learning Gardens, Columbus, Ohio; designed by various designers and staff (www.chadwickarboretum.osu.edu).

Chanticleer Garden, Wayne, Pennsylvania; designed by staff (www.chanticleergarden.org).

Cleveland Botanical Garden, Cleveland, Ohio; designed by staff (www.cbgarden.org).

Cohen Garden, Collegeville, Pennsylvania; owned and designed by Stephanie Cohen.

Cornell Plantations, Ithaca, New York; designed by staff (www.plantations.cornell.edu).

Crockett Garden, Hillsboro, Oregon; owned and designed by Laura Crockett (www.gardendiva.com).

Diemer Garden, Sherman, Connecticut; owned and designed by Kathy Diemer.

Ewing and Muriel Kauffman Memorial Garden, Kansas City, Missouri; designed by staff.

Fellerman Garden, Pawling, New York; owned by Janet and George Fellerman; designed by Tenley Dexter.

Ferguson's Fragrant Nursery, St. Paul, Oregon; owned and designed by Danielle Ferguson (www.fragrantnursery.com).

Fries and Bowers Garden, Portland, Oregon; owned and designed by Susan Fries and Lew Bowers.

Gardens at Northview, Ambler, Pennsylvania; owned and designed by Jenny Rose Carey and Gus Carey.

Gervais and Wotzak Garden, New Milford, Connecticut; owned and designed by Michelle Gervais and Rob Wotzak.

Ginsburg Garden, Roxbury, Connecticut; owned by Barry and Merle Ginsburg; designed by Merle Ginsburg and David Bergman.

Hall-Behrens Garden, Portland, Oregon; owned and designed by Lauren Hall-Behrens (www.lilyvillagardens.com).

Hardiman Garden, Portland, Oregon; owned and designed by Lucy Hardiman (www.lucyflora.com); mosaic walkway created by Jeffrey Bale (www.jeffreygardens.com).

Hollister House Garden, Washington, Connecticut; designed by George Schoellkopf (www.hollisterhousegarden.org).

Jerry Fritz Garden Design project, Ottsville, Pennsylvania; designed by Jerry Fritz (www.jerryfritzgardendesign.com).

Lady McDonald Garden, Portland, Oregon; owned by Susan Bates; developed by Lady Anne Kerr McDonald and Sir James McDonald.

Leonard and DiGiovanni Garden, Thomaston, Maine; owned by Linda Leonard and Phil DiGiovanni; designed by Lee Schneller Sligh (www.leeschneller.com).

Leva Garden, Roxbury, Connecticut; owned by Michael Leva; designed by David Bergman and Michael Leva.

Linden Hill Gardens, Ottsville, Pennsylvania; owned by Jerry Fritz; designed by Jerry Fritz and Nancy Ondra (www.lindenhillgardens.com).

Minnesota Landscape Arboretum, Chaska, Minnesota; designed by staff (www.arboretum.umn.edu).

The New York Botanical Garden, Bronx, New York; designed by staff (www.nybg.org).

Silk Garden, Farmington, Connecticut; owned and designed by Steve Silk (www.clattervalleygardens.blogspot.com).

Sternberg Garden, West Chester, Pennsylvania; owned and designed by Ilene Sternberg.

Terra Nova Nurseries, Canby, Oregon; owned by Dan Heims; designed by Dan Heims and staff (www.terranovanurseries.com).

Thyrum Garden, Wilmington, Delaware; owned and designed by Per and Eve Thyrum; architectural steel container created by Inta Krombolz.

United States National Arboretum, Washington, D.C.; designed by staff (www.usna.usda.gov).

Index

About the Authors

Stephanie Cohen taught herbaceous plants and perennial design at Temple University for more than twenty years and is the former director of the Landscape Arboretum at Temple University in Ambler, Pennsylvania. She is a columnist for *Fine Gardening*, serves on the advisory boards for Green Profit and the Pennsylvania Horticultural Society's Green Scene, and writes for the Blooms of Bressingham Plant Program and *American Nurseryman*. Her monthly show appears on CNN television. She has received awards from Temple University, the Pennsylvania Horticulture Society, and the American Nursery and Landscape Association and has appeared on QVC-TV as the "Perennial Diva." In April of 2005 she became a Temple University Alumni Fellow, the most distinguished award that can be given to an alumna. *The Perennial Gardener's Design Primer* (Storey) received an award from the Garden Writers Association; her most recent book was *Fallscaping*. Stephanie holds undergraduate degrees in English and horticulture and a master's degree in environmental studies. She and her husband have three children and two grandchildren.

After graduating with a bachelor's degree in horticulture from The Ohio State University, **Jennifer Benner** spent a good amount of time getting dirt under her fingernails. She has experience in nursery production as well as garden design, installation, and maintenance. Jennifer eventually landed in Nantucket, Massachusetts, where she worked as a horticulture manager, specializing in perennial and container gardens. In 2001 she joined the staff of *Fine Gardening* magazine, where she spent seven years taking articles from conception to print. As an associate editor, Jennifer enjoyed working closely with gardeners from around the United States and photographing their spaces. She now spends much of her time working as a freelance writer, photographer, and horticulture consultant but can still be found playing in the dirt, cultivating her garden in northwest Connecticut with her husband, Brent. Although she lives in New England, Jennifer still considers herself a Buckeye.